The Fight of My Life

Barbara Clark

The Fight of My Life

With a foreword by Sharon Osbourne

HODDER &
STOUGHTON

First published in Great Britain in 2007 by Hodder & Stoughton
A division of Hodder Headline

The right of Barbara Clark to be identified as the Author of the
Work has been asserted by her in accordance with the
Copyright, Designs and Patents Act 1988.

A Hodder & Stoughton Book

1

The names and identities of some of the people mentioned have been changed in
the interests of their privacy.

Writing by Chris Stevens

A CIP catalogue record for this title is available from the British Library

ISBN 978 0 340 93809 6
ISBN 0 340 93809 9

Typeset in Sabon by M Rules

Printed and bound by
Mackays of Chatham Ltd, Chatham, Kent

Hodder Headline's policy is to use papers that are natural, renewable and
recyclable products and made from wood grown in sustainable forests. The
logging and manufacturing processes are expected to conform to the
environmental regulations of the country of origin.

Hodder & Stoughton Ltd
A division of Hodder Headline
338 Euston Road
London NW1 3BH

Foreword

When you have cancer, you're plunged into a new world. You have to take in new information; become an expert on your own cancer; keep your own spirit alive; you have to be strong for your children. And there's chemo – which for most people becomes like a full-time job. It can be a commitment that means everything else has to take second place. You focus on getting well.

You can never explain to someone who hasn't had chemo, what it's like. On one level it's the most miserable experience. It drains your energy, drains your soul and makes you feel sick as a dog, sick to death. On the other – it saves your life. It's on your side in the battle.

It is so amazing to fight that battle and win. And even more amazing to be in the middle of that battle – and then take on another one, as Barbara Clark has.

I first met Barbara, and her gorgeous little boy Ash, at the Sun Wondermum awards. She stood out for me as my kind of woman. All the women there had done incredible things, but I couldn't believe Barbara's spirit. I am backing her every step of the way.

To have a child who's ill is devastating, as I know. To have cancer would bring anyone to their knees. Barbara's lived through those experiences and then some, but on top of that, she fought the system to get the cure she needed and she won. Only a mother could have been brave enough to do that. Only a mother could fight so hard, not to knock someone else down but to keep herself alive – and to help everyone else who needed it. That's my kind of spirit. That's a woman after my own heart. You put your family first when you're faced with a devastating situation like that, and that's how you do the impossible.

We know now that cancer isn't something you just get when you're old. Young people everywhere are getting it, too often. I know this from my work as part of the Sharon Osbourne Colon Cancer Program. But thank God the treatments are getting younger and newer too – more and more incredible solutions like Herceptin that everybody should have a right to.

There are lots of resources out there for people with cancer. I think one of them should be taking inspiration from people like Barbara who are fighters, survivors, who have taken on something so difficult and pulled it off. I've beaten cancer and I know the courage it takes. I hope reading this book will help give more people out there the courage they didn't know they had.

Sharon Osbourne

Preface

Everything they say, all those clichés, they're true.

My blood ran cold. My stomach turned over. Time slowed down. All of that happened.

My fingers had felt a lump, under my left arm, a growth exactly where the old one had been. That first lump had been cancer and it had come very close to killing me after I discovered it, thirteen months before.

This was a new lump; but it might be the old cancer. It could be the same malignancy, back for a second stab at killing me.

And if that was the case, I was going to die.

I didn't scream. I didn't have to sit down. With my mind surprisingly calm, as if I had been expecting this, I continued to explore the contours of the lump with my fingertips. There were simple questions I needed to ask, to find out my fate: Did this growth move? Was it painful? Was it smooth, or coarse like orange peel?

Raising my elbow to the back of my head, I tried to see the lump from the clearest angles in the mirror, trying to get the light on it. Trying to feel round the back of it, to see if it was solid, immovable and uneven on the underside, as the first lump had been. Cancers tend not to move around – did this? I couldn't be certain.

Finding this new lump had nothing to do with chance. I'd been looking for it because I had survived breast cancer once. I was feeling for lumps minutes after I had come out of the treatment room. It was ridiculous, but I couldn't help myself. I was constantly checking.

People try to offer reassurance, promising that I would move on, that the fear of a recurrence would fade. I hadn't had a chance yet to find out if that was true. It was 16 March 2006, merely a matter of weeks since I'd been given the all-clear, since a mammogram had shown there was no cancer in my breasts.

I turned away from the bathroom mirror. It might have been fluid. It might have been a lymph node. It might have been nothing to worry about; but I was going to worry. I was going to think about nothing else till I knew. The question was, would it help to know? If this was a death sentence, did I want to hear a doctor say it out loud?

I wanted to keep it to myself. But when the nurse came to my home to give me my drugs that lunchtime – the drugs I'd fought for, tooth and nail, in the desperate hope they'd give me a chance of life – I had to tell her. Keeping my voice as calm as I could, I said, 'I've got a new lump. I think the cancer's back. It's going to kill me this time.'

The nurse was composed and sensible. She said exactly what I would have said if I'd been wearing my nurse's uniform that day.

'You have to tell your doctor, Barbara. Straight away.'

If I had to put my life in someone else's hands, Dr Paul Hansford is the GP I would trust. I knew he could be relied on neither to overreact nor to dismiss my fears lightly. I called him and said, 'I'm not sure, but I think my cancer might be back. What should I do? Should I ring the hospital?'

Part of me wanted him to say, 'Don't be silly, Barbara. You can't have another lump. You've only just had the all-clear.'

Instead, his tone was brisk and urgent: 'Come and see me first, right now. You don't need an appointment.'

I turned up just after Dr Hansford finished his morning surgery. After a careful inspection, he announced, 'I think I can detect a lump, too. It may well be nothing, but we know that last time it was – we can't afford any delays with this. I'll write to the hospital, but in the meantime you must ring them and tell them what you found. Get up there and have it checked out.'

I was in shock as I left the surgery. Part of my brain had told me, all the way there, 'This must be your imagination. You know that the constant imagining of lumps is part of what follows cancer.'

The confirmation from Dr Hansford that he could feel something too was as great a shock as the first time I'd been diagnosed. And because the lump was in the same place as before, I was absolutely terrified. In a dazed state, I went home and rang the hospital. They said I could come in on Thursday, which was two days away.

I didn't sleep much in those two days.

Everything I'd been through, everything I'd achieved – the human-rights case, the publicity, the victory over the NHS, the fight of my life – was all that over? Was the cancer really going to win after all? Should I have accepted from the start that the clock was ticking down the last weeks and days of my life?

No. I wouldn't accept defeat until it killed me. That's not me, not my style. I'm a fighter.

Though Taunton Musgrove Hospital didn't have a resident oncologist, or cancer specialist, on its roster, I was able to see the staff-grade doctor in the oncology department. Dr Sarah Bryant had become a familiar face to me during the past year, and I had grown used to her solemn, sympathetic manner. I always think of her as Dr Doom. By that I don't mean she has a death-knell voice, or that she's at all unpleasant. It's just that, with her sad eyes and measured speech, she makes me feel as if my days are numbered . . . and the number isn't in double figures.

Sometimes a doctor with a kindly manner is worse than one who'll stand for no nonsense. Often it's best if somebody says, 'There's nothing to worry about – pull yourself together.' But Dr Bryant looks at me with such sympathy that I can't help thinking, This is it! I've had it!

She studied my lump and said, 'I think you're probably right. We need to get a good look at that. Go for another ultrasound.'

The ultrasound team couldn't fit me in for at least another two weeks. That delay would not necessarily matter: if the lump was my old cancer returned, nothing could save me, not even an ultrasound that same day. But two weeks was a long time to wait for what could turn out to be the worst news of my life.

I decided to make the best of it. I had long ago realised that if I was not destined to enjoy a long life, I would do everything in my power to live a short life to the full. My highest priority would be my family – nothing could be better than time spent with the people dearest to me.

With Easter approaching, we were booked on a caravan break in Exmouth. I was going with my younger son, Ash, who is twelve, as guests of my younger brother, Paul, his partner, Alison, and their son, Scott. Scott is eleven, a great playmate for Ash.

I had to tell Paul and Alison about the lump, but the children didn't know. I couldn't let them have any hint of it. Paul's reaction was to play the danger down: 'You'll be all right.' That's the way he copes, but I knew he was very worried. Alison was a lot more sympathetic – the first thing she did when she got the news from Paul was to phone me and pour out her support.

It was a dreadful situation to be in when you're going off on holiday, but I knew how much the break meant to everyone. I forced myself to smile, and immediately felt better – smiling generates endorphins, or 'happy' hormones. I'm not pretending to be brave; I'm just blessed with brilliant sons who unfailingly keep my spirits buoyant. Richard, my nineteen-year-old, would be working and unable to join us, but Ash was looking forward to this break as if it was the trip of a lifetime. With Ash around, smiling is easy. No matter how frightened I was, it was impossible to go on holiday with my sweet, cheerful little boy and wear a scowl.

Paul had booked and paid for the caravan as his family's holiday. Since there was a spare bedroom, they invited us, which is typical of his generous nature. The caravan site had a spa, where you could sit and bubble away in the

Jacuzzi. Paul thought that would be ideal, and it did turn out to be inspired.

I'm very close to Paul, and have been since he was born. I always wanted a baby boy of my own and, for me, my little brother was the next best thing. He's nine years younger than me and I adored him when we were growing up, though he'll tell you a different story: he'll say that I used to chase him and tickle him, but naturally I deny it. Paul was gorgeous, blond and blue-eyed. I have another brother who is only two years younger, but he didn't like me to fuss over him or spoil him; we were more like friends.

Because there were three adults and two children on our holiday, we could take the Jacuzzi in turns, jumping into the hot tub in pairs, with the third one doing the babysitting. So Paul went in with Alison, and the next day I went in with her . . . That way, she managed to enjoy a double ration of spas. That girl's not daft.

We were fortunate with the Devon sunshine. The Jacuzzi was out on the roof and there were even a few mad people sunbathing, though it wasn't really warm enough. But we sat in the hot tub and it was like being in the south of France. The sea was blue, the sun was shining, it was absolutely fabulous . . . and we sat there and we talked about the lump.

I wasn't thinking too negatively – it wasn't as if I was convinced this would be the last family holiday I'd ever have. I always have hope. I can say without false modesty that I'm a brave person – I've been through enough to know. I can usually rely on myself to find that bit of courage I need.

I told Alison, 'If I have the ultrasound and it goes against me, I'll say, "Will of God," and I'll get on with what's left of my life. My philosophy so far has been "Where there's life there's hope." And if the hope runs out, that philosophy is going to become "Only the good die young"!'

We fell about laughing. What else are you going to do?

But what worried me more than anything was telling the boys. I just couldn't face it. Just a few weeks before, I'd told Ash and Richard that I was clear of cancer. Now I thought of my boys' faces if I had to break the worst to them.

I knew I wouldn't be able to keep it a secret, because I'd be going backwards and forwards to the hospital. I'd need another operation, and the media would certainly pick up on it. I've been very honest with the media right from the start of my campaign, always willing to explain my timetable of appointments and treatments. This was the first time I'd hidden anything from them.

It wasn't that I wanted to deceive anyone, but I was simply terrified of telling my sons.

I said to Alison, 'There are a few possibilities here. It could be a new primary lump, in which case I've still got a chance of getting it removed and being cancer-free. Or it could be the old lump returned, in which case the cancer will be incurable. I might live for years with the right treatment, but the doctors will classify me as terminally ill. It could be delayed by treatments such as chemotherapy, but in the end it will spread. But there is a third possibility: it could be benign. I'm praying that's the case, because it's the one outcome that leaves me with nothing to worry about. Let's face it, nine out of ten lumps are benign. But this one's in exactly the same place as the last one.'

Those were the three possibilities, and we discussed them countless times while we were bubbling away. Curiously, the conversations weren't depressing; in fact, we felt energised and uplifted. Something so grim hanging over your head makes you aware of how good life is.

I sat there and I soaked up the sunshine. I loved the fact that I was alive, and I loved the view. It was sensational. I love living. I grab it with both hands. The knowledge that you might soon be taken away from your family makes you intensely aware of how much you feel for them, and how much you want to spend time with them. Nothing else matters half as much. We didn't even have to stroll over to the clubhouse in the evenings; it was enough to share a bottle of wine in the caravan and reminisce.

Within weeks I was granted a reprieve. The ultrasound, when it eventually came, gave promising signs that my growth was benign, and a triple core biopsy proved I was safe. Final confirmation, though, didn't come until 27 April, and those weeks were among the most nerve-racking of the whole ordeal. The shock had served one good purpose, however: it had focused my mind on telling this story.

As I lay back and let the Jacuzzi waters massage me, I realised for the first time that I had to get everything set down on paper. Ash is mature for his age, but he is not old enough to fully understand what's been happening in these recent months, and Richard has grown up quickly since my diagnosis, but there's so much they both don't know, and one day they will want to. There's a chance I won't be around to tell them.

I started to think about my battle for survival in the context of my whole life. I already understood that, in many ways, my experiences had been preparing me for this for a long time.

Chapter One

I come from a family of strong women. My mother stood out among them, though; an amazing, resilient person. Her influence has made me the campaigner that I am. My father walked out when I was about twenty, leaving her with the half-built foundations for an extension to their house, just outside Epping, in Essex.

I thought she'd have to hire a builder, either that or cover the foundations over and forget about having an extension. Instead, she learned how to lay bricks. She mixed the cement, carted the bricks, even laid the roof, singing 'If You Could See Me Now' as she did it. It took her between eighteen months and two years to complete the work, and I don't think she ever once doubted she'd finish the job.

That's the kind of woman I grew up with. That's the strength which is in my genes. I think about my mother often and I draw a lot of inspiration from her.

I was born in the mid-1950s, in Whipps Cross Hospital, on the edge of Epping Forest, which is in London now but was actually in Essex at the time. There's pure Essex girl in my soul. My parents were Lee and Wally Clark, and I had three younger siblings – brother, brother, sister – Jim, Paul and Alison. I was a big sister from the time I could first talk, and that role sums my character up: you can rely on me to look after the others, but don't ever try to tell me what to do!

I went to Barclay Primary School and Leyton County High for Girls, leaving at sixteen. I have to confess I wasn't an academic overachiever, though it wasn't lack of brains; it was lack of work. I later went on to tackle a degree.

I was always more interested in the real world than in my lessons. Studying wasn't what interested me; enterprise did. I used to sell cosmetics in class. I got my mother to sign up as an Avon rep and I took the catalogues and samples into school. The teachers didn't like it, but I was a little bit of a rebel even then.

By the time the family moved to Epping, I had already left home. It wasn't long before Dad left. I was wrapped up in my own life, so the shock probably didn't hit me as hard as it would have done if I'd been younger. In fact, I'd had a very good upbringing as a youngster and I look back on a happy childhood. From my perspective, my parents hadn't had a difficult relationship. I can't remember any shouting matches or serious rows. It was a calm, happy household.

As I adjusted to life after school, I increasingly felt that I had seen only a tiny sliver of the world. My cousin Christine felt the same way. We wanted to have an adventure. So we went to Germany and worked as laundry maids. It was a package: our tickets and hotel accommodation were provided on condition that we worked in the hotel laundry. I was there for a year, surrounded by cockroaches. It was slave labour, but I thoroughly enjoyed that period of my life. I was only seventeen.

I was working entirely with immigrant labour, mainly Turkish girls, so as I picked up German, I spoke it with a Turkish accent. It used to make the German staff laugh to hear me talk, but of course German was the only language I had in common with the other girls.

When I came back from Germany, I tried a series of jobs. For a while I worked at an outdoor swimming pool, taking entrance money on the desk, and every evening after the pool closed the lifeguards would throw me in. I can remember many sunny afternoons walking through Epping Forest dripping wet. I wasn't a strong swimmer, but I soon learned to swim to the side fully clothed.

In my late teens I met my first husband. His name was Johnny and he was a market trader, with a stall selling shirts and trousers. I used to help on it. I still only have to look at a man and I can size him up. One glance and I say, 'Fifteen and a half shirt collar.'

At first, I had the time of my life. Outdoor work, with the chance to meet lots of people in an informal setting suited me well. My needs were few: top of the list was good weather. If there was a chance to catch the sunshine, I would soak it up from the stall, watching the world bustle by. I can remember one of my old teachers walking past, seeing me and saying, 'Oh, Barbara, has it come to this?' I was a grammar-school girl, in the days when grammar schools thought they were that bit better. But it hadn't 'come to' anything; I was simply enjoying myself. And I was earning more than she did! I've never been terribly conventional.

Johnny and I got married when I was nineteen. Looking

back, I realise that was ill-judged. The best explanation is that I was a hopeless romantic. I was probably also head-strong and too intent on establishing my independence. I was certainly deaf to my mother's good advice that if this relationship was good enough to last a lifetime we had no reason to rush into marriage. But marry we did, and we got a flat together in Leytonstone. I'd known him for just a year. He was my first serious boyfriend, and we were married for just seven weeks. Then he hit me.

I reported him, but this was the mid-1970s and the police were less aware of the impact of domestic violence than they are today. They said, 'Yeah, you'll go back to him.'

I thought, No, I won't.

I never went back. Johnny had hit me, got me round the throat and started strangling me. He wasn't drunk; in fact, the attack happened quite early in the morning. It erupted out of an argument about the washing-up. Ours was a small flat, I was doing the dishes, and he said I was making too much noise. So he came out into the kitchen and slapped me.

I know now that this is the beginning of a pattern in violent relationships, and that it's centred on issues of dominance and control. The dishes and the noise were irrelevant – it could as easily have started over the television or the cooking. At the time, it shocked me to the pit of my stomach. In an instant I had discovered that I didn't know my husband at all.

This was the only warning I needed. I'd never experienced violence and I was determined never to put up with it. I took a change of clothes and my hairdryer, I walked out of that marriage, and I never went back.

Johnny had had a very turbulent upbringing and violence was just the way of life he knew. His sister later told me, 'That's what our family do. That's all we've known all our lives.' He'd been brought up with fists and belt buckles, and violence was how he coped.

My parents never shouted, they never swore, and if they had arguments I never saw them. I was brought up in a quiet, loving atmosphere. Even now I don't like shouting. I can't have an argument and shout: I'd get upset. I've never experienced that sort of relationship. Even when I'm watching television I don't like to see confrontations and violence.

With nowhere to live, I had little choice but to swallow my pride and go back to my mum. She was actually very good about it – to give her her due, she didn't say, 'I told you so.' She was just relieved to have me home. Johnny wasn't the sort of man my mother wanted her daughter to marry. But nobody's all bad, and he was a lot of fun – very entertaining and hysterically funny. He could light up a room and could really tell a joke.

Getting a divorce was easy. After three years I wrote to him and said, 'Is it OK if I go ahead with divorce proceedings, and will you pay half?' He wrote back to agree, so it was a divorce by mutual consent. I sent him a 'happy divorce' card. I can't say I regret marrying Johnny, or have any bad feelings towards him. All my life I've made choices, often in direct opposition to what was expected of me. Sometimes that led to a short-lived disaster, but more often it's given my life its meaning. If I'd always taken the conventional road, I wouldn't have Richard, I wouldn't have Ash, and I probably wouldn't have my life. I'll never regret my choices.

Chapter Two

I've always loved children, especially those with no real family to care for them. In my early twenties I went to America, where I had my first experience as a surrogate mother. I had no idea at the time, but this was a foretaste of my true vocation.

I was twenty-four or twenty-five. I went to Plantation, near Fort Lauderdale in Florida, as an au pair and was also expected to do some work around the father's office. I worked day and night, but I was very much part of the family. The father, Jay, interviewed me in London, and his intention was that I would go out and work with him and his wife, and look after their daughter, Debbie, who was ten. When I arrived in Florida, however, I found the wife had run off with another man and got a quickie divorce – and that was only six weeks later. Only the Americans can work at such speed.

Jay's life was, to put it politely, in a state of flux. To be more blunt, he'd acquired a new partner who was already living with him. Her name was Sherry and she had a daughter, Cameron, who was five. Sherry was extremely pretty, a real-life Barbie doll with a deep-fried Southern accent, and though she displayed a cunning skill for getting the things she wanted, she also made an effort to be absolutely brainless. I was convinced this was an act: nobody can be that stupid without trying.

Jay's own daughter, Debbie, was in a terrible state. She couldn't bear to see her father fawning over his new girl-friend, but most of all she harboured a death wish for Cameron.

It's understandable that she was so jealous and confused. Not only did she have a stranger arriving from England to look after her, but she had to deal with her dad's new girl-friend, who looked like a young Dolly Parton. Debbie's response was quite aggressive. I found myself looking after both her and Cameron, and trying to separate them all the time.

The situation became supercharged when Jay's father moved in. He thought Sherry was a gold-digger, in the rela-tionship for the money. She behaved like a little girl – coy and subservient. She defended herself with simpers: she was from South Carolina, where a lot of women are brought up to be submissive. She used to call Jay's father 'sir'. Jay adored Sherry, but his father couldn't stand her and would shout at her. Jay used to shout back at both of them.

They had some ding-dong, screaming arguments, and of course I wasn't used to it. It reached a head when, at the height of one row, I couldn't hold back my own tears any longer. I was sitting beside the swimming pool, very dis-tressed. Debbie ran to her father and told him, 'Dad, you've got to stop! Barbara's upset.'

He was genuinely puzzled. 'What are you crying about?' he asked me. 'Nobody's shouting at you.'

I said, 'I can't bear it! I can't bear it!'

After about three weeks, Cameron was sent back to South Carolina to live with her grandparents. Her relationship with Debbie was terrible, and, twenty years on, after many years of working with children from broken marriages, I can fully understand how impossible it was for both of them. They were the victims of thoughtless, selfish adults. It left me with a mess to sort out in Debbie's head. She was very distressed, a damaged child – in a matter of six weeks, she'd lost her mum, who had run off to live with her lover on a boat, and was expected to accept her dad's new girlfriend and her child.

I did what I could for her, but I didn't really have much experience of children at that time. Apart from having younger siblings, I had not had an opportunity to develop proper childcare skills. All I could do was to try to be a friend to her, to be there for her. I've learned over the years that often it's all you can do. Some problems can't be fixed, but working through them is easier if there's a supportive adult around who is willing to listen and sympathise without judging.

Debbie certainly found my accent very funny. She used to refer to her 'fanny', meaning her backside, and I'd tell her, 'You can't say that! You have to say "bottom".'

She thought that word was absolutely hysterical, especially with an English accent: 'Bore-tomm!'

I really felt for her. Fortunately, by the time I went back, Sherry had left. I had to return to England because I had become homesick after a year, but things were settling down for them. It was a stressful situation to find yourself parachuted into – absolute chaos, a broken marriage and a child who is traumatised. In the end, I think I was able to help, and make a bad situation more bearable. I can't say I didn't enjoy my first experience of the States – they had a waterbed, in the days when waterbeds were impressive. I wasn't just working for the family; I was very much taken into their hearts. They took me everywhere with them, especially to restaurants, because they used to eat out a lot. Jay couldn't cook, Sherry couldn't cook, I couldn't cook, and we didn't want to starve so we ate out all the time.

One thing that struck me as peculiar was that Jay behaved like a strict father with me. On the one date I had out there, my young admirer had to come in to be questioned. Jay asked about where he came from, almost what his prospects and his intentions were. That was an unsettling experience, and after that date I didn't have another one: I was so embarrassed. But Jay was essentially a sweet-natured man and he felt he had to look after me because I was much younger than him. That was the only way he knew to look after a woman, by being very protective. It was not an unpleasant sensation, but quite foreign to me.

I caught up with the family years later, and Debbie declared I helped her through the toughest months of her life and then showed her how to have fun again. Even now, I rank that small victory very highly. I discovered that I could make other people's lives better, and it was a marvellous, empowering feeling.

Around this time, I also discovered a real empathy towards people who were ill and who needed nursing back to health. It was a calling I had felt since my teens, but it was intensified in my early twenties when I needed a short stay in hospital for a minor operation. That showed me what it was like to need the professional care of a nurse, and how important their work had been to my recovery. I knew I could provide the same care and support to others.

I embarked on nurse's training when I was twenty-seven at Whipps Cross Hospital, where I had been born, and I absolutely loved it. Originally I had applied to Bart's, but there was an eighteen-month waiting list, so I rang round all the local hospitals and the training hospitals on my own initiative, seized with an enthusiasm that simply was not going to be extinguished. Whipps Cross took me on straight away. That was a momentous day: I had decided what I wanted to do with my life. Nursing was my vocation and it was what I'd been born to do.

It's difficult to analyse my decision to go into nursing. I simply knew I'd found my compass course. Perhaps one catalyst was a holiday I'd taken in Australia that year – I loved the place, and would have liked to have stayed. It appealed to the nostalgic in me: parts of Australia, especially Queensland and the Northern Territories, had retained the feel of the 1960s or 1970s. Knowing I'd need a professional qualification if I was to emigrate, I decided to do my training as a nurse in London and then return to Australia to work. That was a plan that never became a reality, though on wet, wintry afternoons in Bridgwater I sometimes catch myself thinking, I ought to be sunbathing on the other side of the planet right now.

I thoroughly enjoyed my nursing training, in all its aspects. But I discovered in my third year I couldn't cope well with the operating theatre. The sight of blood made me feel faint. The first time I took someone for a bronchoscopy, in which they insert a tube into the patient's nose to conduct an internal inspection of the lungs, I passed out. They had to bring me out on a stretcher. Words cannot describe how the other nurses took the mickey out of me.

But I was determined to be a nurse and I returned to the operating theatre. And fainted again. They kept carrying me out, I kept going back in. I managed three of the eight weeks, with a growing fear that I was going to be a liability. The staff were experienced, and naturally they'd seen cases like mine before. They knew what to do, and a role was found for me in eye theatre, cleaning the instruments. That steered me out of trouble, and took me into ophthalmic nursing.

Around this time, my grandmother suffered a stroke, which kept her in hospital for a number of weeks. I was working in the same building and was able to see her every day, watching as she made a gradual recovery.

Every day Gran talked about one of the young volunteers in the rehab unit who was helping to get her back on her feet. It was clear that she was rather taken with him, and I understood why when I met him. Devon was a tall, powerfully built man with a brilliant smile and a caring heart. What struck me most was his sweet nature and the patience he showed with the patients. He was several years younger than me, still at college and was helping out at the hospital over the summer. I didn't intend to go out with him at first, but by the time he went back to his studies, we were seeing a lot of each other. Age seemed unimportant, and I couldn't have cared less about the occasional racist remarks we attracted – if anyone felt the need to comment that Devon was black and I wasn't, that was their problem. He was absolutely bombproof: I never saw him lose his temper. He was tall and slim then; he's roly-poly now, a big bear, but he was always a gentle soul.

By now I was working in care of the elderly. That didn't seem like a significant career decision at the time – most nurses switch between areas of expertise from time to time, as the job demands. But I quickly discovered that this type of nursing suited me well. It didn't involve trips to the operating theatre, and it gave me plenty of time to get to know my patients. Many elderly people need someone who will listen to them, pay attention to their memories and smile at their stories. I found I derived real satisfaction and pleasure from that.

All the separate aspects of my life seemed to fit together. My work fulfilled me, my boyfriend understood how much my career meant, and my future was filled with bright possibilities. When Devon proposed, I accepted enthusiastically, but we agreed we didn't want to rush into marriage. I'd done that before, with disastrous results. Both of us did, however, want a child, and we decided there was no reason to wait before beginning our family. Shortly after my thirtieth birthday, I became pregnant.

That was one of the most wonderful times of my life. The pregnancy went smoothly and I felt filled with a new sense of purpose. My life had an extra layer of meaning. I had always wanted a baby, even as a nine-year-old besotted with my tiny brother, but to have a real human life growing inside me was an awe-inspiring experience. I was also hard at work, because I kept working in a nursing home all through my pregnancy. By eight months I was so fearsomely pregnant that the other nurses didn't want to share the night shift with me, in case my contractions started at 3 a.m.

As I prepared my nest for a new arrival, my bond with my own mother grew stronger. We chatted constantly about her first pregnancy, comparing the way she felt when she was expecting me with what I was feeling. In those long conversations I learned a lot about my background, my mother's family and my early childhood. Suddenly, it was important to me to know where I came from. I instinctively knew it would help me to understand who my baby would be.

Richard was born in London in 1986. I hadn't planned to have him there – he was supposed to be born in Eastbourne, where the nursing home was and where I was living, but on a visit to the capital I went into labour, two weeks early. I had him at Whipps Cross Hospital; one of my school friends, a qualified midwife, performed the delivery.

Devon was with me for the birth, and I could see, even in those draining days, that he wasn't himself. I tried to put it down to the emotional strain of becoming a father, but it was quickly obvious that there was something serious on his mind. When I challenged him, three days after the birth, his answer devastated me: 'I can't stay with you, Barbara. I've met someone else. We couldn't help it – we've fallen in love.'

I could hardly speak. He left me in the maternity ward, with the car in the car park and a three-day-old baby. I had

had a Caesarean and was unable to drive myself home. My brother Paul had to come and pick us up.

Tiny though he was, and completely unaware of the emotional trauma all around him, Richard helped me get through the next few weeks. Being a mother changes everything you are. My self-image, my whole identity, was transformed. I could not imagine loving anyone more than I loved my child. Beside that, the feelings I had for Devon were less important, and his claim to be 'in love' was selfish and trivial. With a child to care for, I knew I could cope with anything – because if I stopped coping, how would my darling boy fend for himself? He needed me to be strong, and through that need he gave me strength.

Devon and I never got back together, but our friendship survived. I forced myself to get over the break-up because the only truly important thing was that Richard should grow up knowing his dad. I felt very bitter and angry for about two years, but in the end there are more important things than broken hearts. I'm an adult.

That is not to belittle the difficulty of those early years. I had not planned to be a single mother. Three weeks after Richard was born, I returned to work. I didn't have a choice: this was a matter of putting food on the table. As soon as I'd had my stitches out, I went back to work in the nursing home, a family-run concern. I used to walk around with Richard in a sling on my back and the old folk loved it. Whatever I had to do, washing people or helping them into bed, Richard was there with me. He saw more naked women in his first six months than he'll probably see in the rest of his life.

Regulations are tighter today than they were then: I wouldn't get away with bringing a child to work every day now, but in a family-run nursing home, there was more leeway. As Richard grew I used to put him in a baby-walker and he'd trundle round the lounge. The elderly people adored him and would chat to him as he rolled from one to another, with a helping hand reaching out to guide him away from the furniture. He had so many fans – everyone loves a baby and he was really cute. Every new mum feels like that, but there was something special about Richard.

I worked there until Richard was about four, and the experience helped to form his character. He still has clear memories of those afternoons and how he used to answer the bell and fetch glasses of water or orange juice, pass a pair of glasses to a lady who couldn't reach or fetch the newspaper for an elderly gentleman who found it difficult to get out of his chair. To Richard, it was fun. People might say the workplace is no setting for a child, but I believe it was the best thing I could have done for him. He was part of a big family, learning respect and how to be helpful, and being rewarded with friendship and love. He says that to this day, whenever he washes his hands, he does it the way that old Mr Smith, one of the residents, showed him. Mr Smith passed away long ago, of course, but he's remembered by a young man who learned a small but important lesson from him.

It was only possible to take Richard to work with me because the home was so well run. I grieve today when I read of soulless 'care homes' that are like factories where the elderly are processed. In some of these places, there is no sense of family, yet that is what the elderly need more than anything.

Around this time I was briefly married for the second time. The relationship didn't work out, largely because my husband had devout religious beliefs that I respected but couldn't share. I had hoped that would not be an obstacle to our love, but ultimately it was.

Now, my ex-husband is a friend and when I was diagnosed with breast cancer last year, I rang him. His reaction was so positive and encouraging I was buoyed up for days: 'Gosh,' he said, 'you sound like you're coping with it really well. I wouldn't have thought you could deal with it as well as you are. If you need any help, I'm here for you.' That's the kind of frankness and support you can only get from someone you've known a long time, someone who appreciates where the roots of your personality lie. There's a directness between you that you won't find with newer friendships.

When you have a major diagnosis of illness such as cancer, you're suddenly surrounded by people in a similar situation and by professionals who have deep experience of combating the disease. Their support and expertise is vital, but in a way it is also superficial. The doctors and the new comrades in your cancer support group don't know you all the way through. They haven't shared your life for years.

The only people with that deep knowledge are your friends and family. That's why I'd urge anyone who is going through a break-up to hold on to the friendship. You might have to let the relationship go, you might not be sharing a bed any longer, but don't let that be a death sentence for the friendship. Hang on to your friends, because the time will come when you need them, or they need you.

As Richard was growing up, I applied that rule to my relationship with Devon. Part of me wanted to slam the door on those memories and never go near them again. That might have made my own life a little bit easier, but it would have made my son's ten times harder. I had no right to pursue a feud with Devon, because Richard needed that relationship. Devon had left me for another woman, which hurt, but looking back, I know that he genuinely had fallen in love. It happens. Ultimately, though, it wasn't to last.

Devon then met his current partner, Rita, who works in childcare. They've got two lovely children, and I've invited them down for a holiday this year. It took me years to get over our break-up, but Devon is now part of my family. He feels the same way. Rita has always been kind to Richard, and I've always got along well with Devon's mum.

Richard and Ash regard Devon and Rita's children as their brother and sister. When I want to go to London, Devon and Rita put me up. She is several years younger than him, and of course I'm older than him, so I'm like a mother to her.

When I was first facing up to the diagnosis of breast cancer, Devon was a rock: 'Is there anything I can do, Barbara? We're family. We're all together.' That meant so much to me, because at that time I needed all the help I could get.

Chapter Three

One sunny afternoon when Richard was about five, I took him on an outing to Brighton Pier and a new chapter in my life began. I had left care of the elderly and was working as a school nurse. We were living on the south coast, near Hastings. The job involved some child-protection duties, and gave me a mixture of responsibility and hands-on care, which I found intensely fulfilling. Children responded to me and seemed to trust me, and I in turn loved them. Richard was still very little, and I found myself studying the older children, the miniature grown-ups of nine or ten, and observing them as I taught them health education. Some of them came from broken homes and deprived backgrounds, and I had an urge to mother them. An idea started to grow that one day, perhaps when Richard was fully grown, I would become a foster parent to children with special needs. It seemed a long way off, though – somehow I couldn't imagine it would happen before I was fifty.

As Richard and I queued on the pier that day to ride the miniature rollercoaster, I couldn't help watching the two sweet girls in front of us. One of them was about my son's age, the other a little older. They and the man with them were smiling because they had picked up on Richard's eagerness to go on the ride and my reluctance. Actually, 'reluctance' isn't a strong enough word; I was petrified. Even travelling more than 50 miles per hour in a car turns my legs to jelly, and at a fairground the coconut shy is about as much thrill-seeking as I can handle.

Richard was holding me in the queue by clinging on to my arm with both hands, but every time we took a step closer to the ticket booth my knees knocked harder. 'Come on, Mum,' he was pleading. 'You'll love it.' Years later, when he was working up the courage to make a parachute jump, I reminded him of that scene. But that afternoon, I think I would have been happier to step out of an aeroplane than on to the rollercoaster.

The man with the two young girls came to my rescue. 'Would you like me to take him with us?' he asked.

I gratefully pressed Richard's fare into his hand and retreated to watch them from the sidelines. Later, as the children tucked into ice creams, the man told me that his name was Robert and that he was a car salesman and a divorcee. What struck me immediately was what a caring father he was. I had seen a few of the dads at the school I worked at and it seemed to me they fitted into two basic categories: the ones who thought childcare was beneath them, and the ones who treated their children as the most precious people in their lives. Robert was definitely a life-long subscriber to the second group.

The following week, the five of us met for a long walk across the Downs. Richard and the two sisters, Jennifer and Helen, played together so happily it was easy for Robert and I to start to get to know each other. Often it's easier to look after three youngsters than a single one because they'll keep each other entertained. Teasingly, I called the girls 'the Laura Ashley sisters' because they loved flowery dresses. They lived with their mother during the week, but Robert was able to spend most weekends with them, and he didn't waste a minute of that time. Both of us had been hurt before, so the relationship proceeded cautiously, but after a year Richard and I moved in with Robert in West Sussex.

My outlook on relationships is simple: I want to be committed and loyal, and I expect the same from my partner. It's about trust, openness and shared emotions. By this time I had realised that I feel more comfortable in a relationship when I'm not constricted by marriage. I think not everyone is suited to it. For some people, marriage is a comforting duvet of security; to me, it's a pillow over my head. I feel there's an obligation about marriage – it's about getting the dinner on the table and having to fulfil the role of a wife.

We lived together for several years, but around 1996 my mother and Robert's father both became ill. Robert is the youngest, by several years, of three siblings, and his parents were elderly. His mother could not cope with her husband's increasing health and mobility problems, and Robert had to devote a lot of his free time to caring for them. That didn't affect our relationship in itself – I admired his dedication and capacity for love – but it did mean that when my own mother started to suffer serious heart problems on her farm in Cornwall, there was no way Robert could leave his parents and move with me to the West Country to care for her.

Richard was eleven when we moved to the Devon–Cornwall border. He was about to start secondary school so the timing was good. Robert and I continued to see each other at weekends and called each other daily. It put emotional pressure on us, but we both accepted that these situations are inevitable when family commitments become demanding. I wouldn't have had it any other way – the reason I'd fallen for Robert in the first place was his unselfish love for his family.

There was no school nursing service where I was in Cornwall, so I took a job in a general ward in an ordinary hospital. My contact with children was limited, though I did help to run the local Beaver group. The hospital work wasn't inspiring, however, and I rapidly knew that general nursing was no longer what I wanted to do. Throughout my career I had specialised – first in opthalmic care, then in homes for the elderly and then, just before Richard was born, I was working in both genito-urinary nursing and HIV care. It was during the latter period that I had discovered my one limitation as a nurse: I become too easily involved in the emotional side of the work. I can't switch it off and it becomes exhausting.

In the mid-1980s, when I had worked in HIV care, HIV had a very high mortality rate. It doesn't now, thanks to anti-retrovirals and the combination of other drugs that can enable people to live a full life. But in those days, patients died, and such was the hysterical prejudice in the media that nobody wanted to touch people with HIV. There was a lot of ignorance about how the disease was spread. The nurses were the last line of emotional defence, and very often I would hug my clients, or sit and hold their hands. Some of them became close friends. And when my friends died, I found it hard and became distressed by it. I couldn't keep taking the pressure that came with the work, which was why I had decided to move into school nursing. Now that I was in Cornwall and couldn't work in school nursing, I had no desire to churn up those old emotions. Working on the wards would not suit my temperament.

My mother and I talked this over. 'You've said to me, more than once, that you plan to be a foster carer in your fifties,' she said.

'I'm not there quite yet, Mum,' I retorted.

'But why wait? If it's what you want, why not do it now?'

It was as if a light came on inside my mind. I'd known people through my work in schools who'd fostered children, and I had the utmost admiration for them. I could see myself in their situation, enjoying the emotional rewards as well as putting in that hard work.

I thought, Why am I waiting till I'm fifty? Live life now! So I contacted the council and started my foster training.

Because I was a nurse, the local authority very quickly picked me out. 'We've got one little boy who we would desperately like to place with a long-term carer. He has severe medical needs, his mum has died, and his father is too distraught to care for him. Is there any chance we could tell you more about him?'

'Absolutely!' I said.

And that was the first time I ever heard Ash's name. He was to change my life in every way imaginable.

It was the spring of 1998, and Ash, who was four, was in foster care in London. He was registered with the Cornish authorities because his father was living in the county,

though his mum had come from Morocco. Ash was already
with a temporary carer, but needed a permanent placement.
I am not a trained paediatric nurse, but I'd worked with
children for years as a school nurse. Now here I was, training to be a foster carer. The local authority must have
thought I was heaven-sent, but to their credit they didn't try
to twist my arm. All the pressure came from my side: I
quickly made up my mind.

Ash was tiny when I met him, the size of a two-year-old.
He'd had a cough all his life, a dreadful hacking cough, and
it was clear he was desperately poorly, but my first thought
was how achingly appealing he was. He was all eyes, enormous brown eyes with long eyelashes. And the boy behind
those eyes looked so frail and frightened.

Ash's temporary foster carer brought him to meet me
four times at the Social Services offices in London, and
every time we parted he cried his eyes out. I felt awful as I
promised him, 'Don't worry, I'll see you again soon.' I just
wanted to picked him up, hug him close and tell him I'd
never let him out of my sight again. Fostering isn't as simple
as that, but how can a four-year-old understand the layers
of bureaucracy and paperwork?

Gradually I understood that the death of Ash's mother
had created some significant psychological problems,
including a severe separation anxiety. Ash was crying
because any separation stirred the unthinkable pain of
being orphaned. For the next three or four years, he would
sob at every parting, from anybody. If a social worker came
for half an hour and was friendly to him, Ash would howl
when she left.

During our first meeting, his temporary foster carer explained about separation anxiety: 'It can be quite embarrassing,' she said. 'When people leave he tries to cling on. He can't talk very well but you know he's begging them to stay. They look at him and wonder what he's going through, as if he's being mistreated behind closed doors. It's a well-known syndrome in children who have been moved around or who have suffered trauma.'

It was plain that Ash had a real need for stability. If I took him on, there could be no going back.

Richard and our dog, Buddy, went with me for my first meeting with Ash, and we've got some photos showing us together, an embryonic family. Ash was a beautiful child and he still is. It was love at first sight, but it took several months to get him back to Cornwall. I went to London every two weeks, and then Ash went into hospital to have some teeth removed. Two weeks later his temporary foster mum brought him to Cornwall, with some of his family and the social worker, en masse. They stayed in a bed and breakfast.

During the intervening weeks, I had discussed the situation in detail with Richard, Robert and my mother. I knew what a serious commitment I was about to make, but I had to convince my family that I understood what I was getting into.

'If it's what you truly want,' Robert said, 'I'll support you all the way. But first of all you'll have to make me believe it really is what you want.'

He knew how much I wanted another child, and we weren't able to have one together. What worried him was the sheer heartbreak that caring for Ash could involve. 'What if his health gets worse?' Robert asked. 'What if you lose him?'

'That's a risk every parent faces,' I said. 'We just can't bear to think about it most of the time. I can't let fear stop me. Ash needs a mother. He's going to carry on living in this world whether I look after him or not, but the difference is, if I turn my back on him now, who's going to love him? Is he going to be left all alone, when I've got so much love to give?'

Robert made one last effort to play devil's advocate, though I think that by this point, secretly, he would have been upset if I had changed my mind. 'Barbara,' he said, 'if you see a documentary about a famine on the other side of the world, you're burning with the urge to fly out there and rescue a refugee camp full of starving kids. Ask yourself, is that what's happening now?'

'I can't save the whole world,' I answered, 'but I can save this one little boy. And that's what I'm going to do.'

The local authority rushed my training through so I could have Ash. Social Services had been looking out for someone like me, because I was a nurse and he had a life-limiting illness, a rare lung condition. With the proper care and a demanding regime of drugs, we hope that he will live well into adulthood, but when he was a small child it was a question of day-to-day survival.

The handover went well. Ash would spend a few hours with me, then a few hours with his old foster family at the bed and breakfast, then a night with me and so on. But after he'd been living with me full-time for about a week, he showed the depth of his confusion when he announced, 'I want to go and live with the next lady now.'

Although he was four, his language skills were underdeveloped and his thinking was often muddled. He didn't understand death; he just knew his mum had gone away and wasn't coming back. I told him, 'Mummy didn't mean to leave you. She loved you very much, and so do I. You've got two mummies who love you,' and then he'd say, 'No, I've got three,' thinking of his previous foster carer.

Sometimes the boys would be watching television together and Ash would start to cry and say, 'I want my mum.' Richard would call out to me and Ash would say, 'Not her – Mum.' We had to work out whether that was his previous foster mother or his real mum: he simply didn't possess the language to explain himself. It was traumatic – the tears I shed every day would have filled a bucket, because I was going through his grief as well. And I couldn't make it better.

It was in June 1998 that Ash came to live with Richard and me, and he was five the following October. If I had not taken the decision to become a foster carer at just the moment I did, our lives would not have been brought together. I think it was meant to be.

Not everyone agreed. The deepest West Country isn't the best place in England to be a single white mother with two mixed-race children. Ash's health problems made things worse.

He has got excellent coordination now, but when I first knew him he was going everywhere in a pushchair. He was a poor walker and dragged his left leg behind him. He'd had a degree of brain damage, a side effect of his lung disorder, which had left him with very poor coordination. To meet him now, you'd never guess that: after years of physiotherapy he's a graceful boy who has won medals for his ability in Latin-American dance. He is also a talented ice-skater.

The first time he saw a physiotherapist was with me, but before long I was doing physiotherapy with him about five times a day. When he came to me, he was in nappies and I was told he was a special-needs child who would always be incontinent. I had him out of nappies in days. I don't think anyone had even tried.

I'm not afraid to share the credit for Ash's progress. He's grown into a normal, physically able child, and that's down to his own determination and my positive attitude. We developed a bond that outsiders could not seem to understand. Some of the professional advice we had was worse than useless: during one visit to a psychologist, Ash said, 'My mummy is in heaven,' which was what his dad had taught him. I believe that's a comforting and positive outlook for an orphaned child, but the psychologist insisted it was wrong to put ideas of heaven into a child's head. There might not be a heaven and I shouldn't be filling Ash's head with these ideas, she claimed. Sometimes I think psychologists don't know what they're talking about.

It has nothing to do with religion: my pragmatic belief is that it helps Ash to know his mummy is in heaven with God and the angels. Even now that he's twelve, we still talk about her as an angel. Last year, we went to the park in Taunton on Mother's Day and released a helium balloon with a tag tied to it that said, 'I love you, Mum. From Ash.' We also plant a flower or a tree every Mother's Day. I don't have a lot of information about Ash before I met him: I don't know what day his mother's birthday was, so Mother's Day is particularly significant for him. One of the plants is a rose, which we have in a pot by the front door and which blooms year after year. If I go on holiday, I give it to a neighbour to look after, because it's so important to Ash. He's always checking it and telling me, 'My mum's rose is flowering again.'

I feel in a way that is hard to explain that Ash's mother watches over us. Everything I have heard about her has been positive. She was clearly a kind and loving woman, and I don't see anything wrong in telling her son that she's in heaven. There have been nights when he's been really bad with his chest, racked with coughs; I'd be sitting up with him at 3 a.m. and I just felt she was watching over us. People can accuse me of being mad if they like, but I found that helpful.

Ash continued to see his father, and their relationship was making encouraging progress. There was other good news: Robert's family situation changed, he got a well-paid job as a senior salesman for BMW in Exeter, and he was able to move down to join us. His daughters were able to come and stay at weekends, too. What's more, a minor medical procedure turned out to be the simple solution to Mum's heart worries. She's been very well ever since.

Mum says she's as old as her tongue and a little older than her teeth. If you press her for her age, she'll tell you she's twenty-one and she's always been twenty-one. She's never admitted to being a day older. That's like me – I'm forty-nine and I've managed to stay that way for two years running.

Unfortunately, racism and prejudice were making our family life impossible. As soon as Ash started going to school, his disability and his family background stirred up a lot of spite and malice. I was shocked – I'd never encountered prejudice like it. I didn't realise people could be so small-minded and vicious.

Ash was tiny and vulnerable. He was no threat to anyone. But the whispers and the sideways glances turned to outright bullying. We started to get racist hate mail. I've still got one of the letters. I kept it as a reminder of what Ash and I have had to face together . . . as if Ash doesn't have enough to cope with, without racial discrimination.

Ash was miserable in school. One afternoon he came home and said to me, 'I want to be human like the other children.' It broke my heart.

I was struggling to cope with Ash's illness, which was physically exhausting me and taking a heavy emotional toll as well. To feel that the whole world hated us was too much. I believe the strain probably caused my cancer, though that's not something I want to dwell on. To think about that too closely would be horrendous.

After enduring it for two years, I decided we had to make a fresh start. The upheaval caused a lot of problems, but staying where we were was not an option. I'm a fighter and I don't readily walk away, but this kind of prejudice wasn't anything I could fight. It was more like a festering sore, something that would only get worse if I touched it.

We decided to move to Bridgwater, in Somerset. There were lots of reasons: I liked Somerset; there was a super school for Richard; property was affordable; and Robert could still commute to his work in Exeter. His job with BMW was too good to lose.

Robert and I were emotionally close, and he was a terrific dad to both Richard and Ash. He would have liked us to be married. I did love him, but I didn't want to get married again. I'd like to be half of a partnership, but I have to be able to maintain my independence within that. I've got a strong personality, though I like my men to be strong, too. I have to respect the man I am with. I'm definitely no feminist, even though I am a powerful female personality. Robert was a strong personality, but he was also quite happy to let me do whatever I wanted.

We bought the house in Bridgwater together, but as time passed it became evident that Robert wasn't coping. His job was putting him under a lot of pressure and he had real problems with the travelling: it was about an hour each way – and anyone who knows the M5 that runs down to Devon will know it's a road that could drive anyone out of their mind. The long distances involved every day placed intolerable pressure on our relationship.

For Robert, I think the real nail in the coffin came in the summer of 2002. I'd had an invitation to visit friends in Nebraska. The flights were affordable and there was nothing to stop me – I had stopped fostering completely to look after Ash. Richard could come with us, as he was on his school holidays. Robert couldn't take any more time off work, but Ash wasn't going back to school till the end of the summer, and I made a spontaneous decision: we're going.

So I left Robert with a list of jobs: drop the dog off at kennels, pick the dog up before we come back, food's in the freezer. Robert was not pleased, and it brought him to a kind of emotional crisis. I had been worried about him for quite a long time, because he kept on saying how unhappy he was. He used to go on and on, and I'm afraid I stopped listening to him in the end.

And then one day, not long after I'd got back from the holiday, he just left. He said, 'I can't cope with this any more,' got in the car and simply drove off. I thought he was going to harm himself because he was so unhappy and he'd been like that for such a long time.

I looked frantically through his stuff, trying to work out where he might have gone. I rang up his mother to tell her how concerned I was about him. She said, 'I wouldn't worry if I were you.'

Hmm, I thought. Why shouldn't I worry? She certainly didn't sound too distraught. I suspected she knew something I didn't, so I went through his stuff again and found a phone number. I rang it and was connected to Disneyland Paris. Clearly this wasn't the worst sort of crisis you could have.

To this day Robert insists that he needed time out with his daughters from his previous marriage. I was hurt that he hadn't invited us too. But it was obvious that he was very unhappy, he couldn't cope with the commuting and the family problems, and he wanted out.

The break-up left me in a terrible mess emotionally and

financially. I bought the house from Robert: one thing about him is he's straight as a die with money. We split everything fifty-fifty. We didn't have a particularly big mortgage, because there were two of us and he had put a lot of capital into the house. However, taking it on alone was a real financial strain.

To add to my money problems, Richard was boarding at a state school, Brymore Agricultural School, in Cannington. He was in his last year of education and was seriously into rugby. He'd always lived at home, but by the time he was fifteen or sixteen he'd decided he wanted to board. It was sport, sport, sport with him, and boarding made life easier – I didn't have to keep picking him up late at night from school, while Ash needed to get to bed.

However, boarding fees, even when they are state rather than private, are a hefty amount each month when you don't have a big income. And I barely had any income. I thought of fostering more children on a short-term basis, which would at least help to make ends meet, but when I had moved from Cornwall to Somerset I hadn't transferred my registration: my name was still on Cornwall's books. It didn't make sense, but local authority regulations often don't. I decided to retrain, but it would take time.

I didn't think life could get much tougher, which shows how much I knew. My relationship was over, my elder boy was boarding at some expense and really didn't want to leave, my younger son had a life-limiting illness, and I was faced with trying to raise the cash to buy my own home when my means of earning a living were in a mess.

I thought I was going to have to downsize to a flat, but a

friend recommended a clever mortgage broker called Brian from Somerset Mortgage Brokers. I renamed him 'St Brian' – he managed to get me a mortgage when nobody else could and enabled me to stay in my home.

I then approached the Haberdashers' Foundation, a charity that helps families with boarding costs for the GCSE year, and they assisted us with the fees for the rest of Richard's final year. He was playing up a lot at the time – he was a pretty horrible teenager, as they all can be. We were going through all sorts of hell with the break-up, and all the accompanying worries and difficulties, and Richard considered Robert to be his dad. Robert had brought him up, so he missed him terribly and acted up.

Ash was playing up, too, but he was so much younger than Richard that it wasn't such an issue. When it comes to giving you a hard life, there's no one to match a teenage boy.

He really was determined to be the teenager from hell. Looking back, I can count my blessings and be thankful that he never got into trouble with the police. At the time, there was no question of counting blessings. He was being thoroughly awkward.

The only time I could see the boy inside the teenager, the person I knew he really was, was when he was playing with the dog. He'd hug and cuddle Buddy. 'Who's my little baby? I love you and we all love you.' That was how I knew Richard was still in there. And then he'd turn round and say something like, 'Grunt, grunt, grunt.'

I won't put up with being shown disrespect, but I had to let it go. I'd seen this from other viewpoints, though I'd never expected to go through it myself: when I was a school nurse, I'd had people ring me up and plead, 'My teenager's awful.'

My advice was always the same: 'Stick it out, they'll come back to you. If they've had a good upbringing, they might be difficult for a few years, but they'll always come back.'

Now I had to take my own advice. Richard was horrible right up to the time I was diagnosed with cancer, and then, instantly, he became a man. That broke my heart. He grew up overnight.

Ash was giving me problems of a different sort. When I first brought Ash out of hospital, I was merely his foster carer and I had to get written permission from his father for any medical procedures he needed. That applied to every injection, every tablet. I couldn't even give the OK for a filling in a tooth. Even for a school trip I would have to get authorisation from Social Services, which was a nightmare.

On top of that, I couldn't take him out of the country without written permission. These things caused problems, because Ash's dad isn't always able to deal with applications and paperwork. The crisis came when Ash went into hospital in Bristol for an operation and the registrar pointed out the consent form hadn't been signed properly. A social worker had to dash round to Ash's dad's house in Cornwall and get him to sign it and then they had to fax it back.

That was a warning to us, and it was intensely frustrating, too. So his dad told me, 'I'd rather you had a residence order,' and I leaped at the chance. Most people might not know what this means – everyone knows about fostering, which means being a temporary short-term or long-term carer, and adoption, which is permanent. A residence order is an alternative to adoption that can work well when one or both of the child's birth parents is still alive and still wants to be involved.

Ash's dad loves him, but he is unable to care for him. He didn't want to give up all his parental rights. The residence order was a smart compromise: it means he'll live with me until he's eighteen, though of course Ash can live with me for as long as he wants. I get parental rights, but I share them with his dad.

That suited everyone. Ash's dad knew I needed those rights to provide Ash with the best care; without parental rights, I needed paperwork to be able to do anything. As far as Ash is concerned, it's basically like an adoption. I'm his official mum and legal guardian – which I would be in my heart, no matter what the pieces of paper said. His dad retains a parent's legal rights, but I've got slightly more say, though there are things I can't do, such as changing Ash's religion. In fact, Ash chooses not to be religious at the moment, like so many twelve-year-olds. He may choose to take up religion again, but he doesn't want that just now.

I can't change his surname, which I wouldn't want to do, anyway. I can't take him out of the country for more than a month; though, having said that, if I needed to go some-where for six weeks or two months, his dad would be fine about it. But I would have to get permission, so I can't go and live in Spain, for instance. It's a good thing I don't want to!

To all intents and purposes, I have a mother's rights. If

Ash needs an operation, or if he needs dentistry work done, that's up to me. But there's a heavy financial cost. A foster carer is a paid carer. When I became Ash's second mum, I was granted a residence-order allowance, but that isn't very much: it's a paltry amount that covers clothing and basic needs. It's nothing like what a foster carer is paid for a special-needs child.

It was like an adoption, and it was a huge financial sacrifice. Do I care? No, because I have Ash. I don't think any of my life would have panned out the way it has if I'd valued money over the people I love.

Chapter Four

It's difficult to bring up a family on a restricted income, but millions of families manage every day. We cope by helping each other. The kindness and support of our friends makes life smoother, and Ash and I have been lucky with our friends. Ash is such an endearing and cheeky lad that he makes good friends easily. Plus, nothing scares him, so I shouldn't have been surprised the day he introduced himself to a superstar and we made two famous friends.

Ash loves music and he loves dance. He's a born popstar, too, and even at seven years old he knew that if there was any justice in life, he'd have a string of number-one hits to his name. Slim, delicate and dark-skinned, he regards himself as Michael Jackson's better-looking little brother, and he loves *Thriller* and the Jackson 5 hits.

When Ash was seven, we heard that Michael Jackson was visiting the West Country, to appear at Exeter City Football Ground. Ash was determined to see him. This wasn't a concert; the football club was run at the time by a consortium that included Uri Geller as its figurehead, and Michael was a friend of Uri's. He'd even been best man at the Gellers' wedding earlier that year.

Apparently, Uri had talked Michael and another friend, the magician David Blaine, into making a personal appearance at the stadium. Our local hospice arranged for a group of sick children to be taken to the ground, and just before Michael arrived, the children were escorted on to the field. Ash was in the front row.

I was at the back of the stands with my instant camera, hopping up and down, trying to take a photograph over people's heads. Michael Jackson was driven on to the pitch. He jumped out of the car, and the next thing I saw was my little Ash, who had quite a bad limp at the time, tearing across the pitch. He'd broken through the security cordon by slipping between a guard's legs.

Ash threw himself into Michael Jackson's arms. Sheltering under a bodyguard's black umbrella, Michael carried him across the pitch – not that he had a choice, because Ash had him in a death grip. I was cheering and clapping.

And then Michael Jackson put Ash down and patted him on the head and said, 'I love you.' It was the best moment of Ash's entire life. He still says he has dreams of all the flash-bulbs going off. We've only got one photograph of him, though, because we couldn't find out who all those photographers were and we never saw any pictures in the press. Still, it made a beautiful memory.

One of the hospice staff told me she knew the young man who had held the umbrella over Michael Jackson. He was a local man named Matt Fiddes, and although he was only in his early twenties, he was building up a chain of martial-arts schools all over the country. He was also a close friend of Michael's. He was supposed to protect his employer from overexcited fans, but despite being one of the UK's best martial-arts teachers, he wasn't quick enough to stop Ash.

Because we didn't have a proper photo or an autograph as a souvenir, I wrote to Matt the next day explaining who we were and asking rather cheekily if he could get a signed photograph of Michael Jackson for us.

Matt was very sweet and got in touch with Uri Geller. Then he called us to say, 'I'll do my best to get a photo signed for you, and Uri says, would you like to go to his mansion and meet him?'

It was a long journey for a poorly boy, but Ash was so excited he wouldn't have missed it for the world – and he wasn't disappointed. The Berkshire mansion lay at the end of a long drive, behind huge electronic gates, with a helicopter pad beside the River Thames. A bit different from our house in Bridgwater. Ash was awed.

Matt was there, and when we'd said our hellos, Uri bent a spoon for Ash, which made his jaw drop. Then Uri took the time to tell me with complete sincerity that he would always be around to give support to my family. And he's been as good as his word.

Matt took Ash outside and showed him some martial-arts moves. Later he told me his karate classes would help Ash to improve his balance and build his self-esteem. 'I think he needs to be a black belt,' he said.

I said, 'I'd love him to, but I just don't have that kind of money.' Matt runs a good school, but of course there are fees.

Matt promised he would have a word with one of his teachers, Ian Hooper, and the upshot was that Ian offered to give Ash lessons for free. He's had years of lessons, with Matt providing the uniforms and kit right the way through and Ian doing the teaching for no payment. The constant generosity of both these men brings tears to my eyes every time I think of it.

Ash came on in leaps and bounds. Martial arts taught him to walk properly and balance. Ian tutored him all the way through to a black belt under the disabled programme. The effect it had on him mentally was remarkable.

Matt also does a lot of work with children's charities. Ash thinks he is a real hero, because he's a martial-arts expert, good-looking, has a ponytail and is very tall – he regards Matt as Superman. Which he is.

That's one of the most striking examples of how kind people have been to us. The people who have supported us have been tremendous. And sometimes a great source of support comes from giving help to others. When my fostering registration had been sorted out in Somerset and I had completed my retraining, I knew that what I wanted most of all was to provide respite care for children with disabilities. That would mean looking after youngsters with severe physical needs or profound learning difficulties, or both, so that the rest of the family could get a break. Without respite care, many parents with seriously ill children never get a holiday or even the chance to enjoy a leisurely evening with a meal and a bottle of wine. Such a situation places appalling pressure on families, and if a respite carer can step into the breach for a few days, it provides a rest for everyone.

Looking back over my life now, I realise my first taste of

caring for children came when I was in America looking after Debbie. Her family had plenty of money, but money doesn't help much when your emotions are going through the wringer.

While I was waiting for a disabled child whom I could care for on a regular basis by providing respite, I started providing short-term placement. This was a new experience for me, and I found it fascinating and exhausting in equal measure. Fresh faces arrived on my doorstep in rapid succession, many of them with severe behavioural problems. They came to stay for as long as two weeks or as little as a weekend. A few returned for a second break, and three or four came to me for several weekends, but most were birds of passage who stopped off for a few days and then went on. Life was sometimes chaotic, but always fun. I had groups of children, at times as many as four at once, as well as individuals.

I was determined to make the fostering work, partly because it was a way of earning enough to provide for Richard and Ash without skimping on Ash's emotional and medical needs, and partly because every child was a fresh challenge. I knew that one day a child could turn round and say, 'I don't feel you tried your hardest with me,' and I did everything in my power to make sure that never happened. Because I was earning again, it meant I could keep Richard on at his school.

Until I got cancer, I used to foster every other weekend, caring for children who were from eighteen months to thirteen or fourteen years old. I'd love to fill this book with my experiences as a carer, but obviously I can't talk about individual cases. Some exhibit extremes of behaviour; some of them have medical needs. My philosophy is to cope with whatever comes up as and when it happens. Some of the children are really draining. The behavioural difficulties can be utterly intense, a reflection of the abuse and neglect they have suffered. Parents who have experienced only the everyday tantrums and traumas of the teen years can be left speechless by their behaviour.

I've had to contend with stealing, soiling, foul language and abuse, threats of violence, destructive behaviour; I've even had to fend off objects hurled at me – without ever losing my temper or allowing my feelings to show. Many of the children smoke, they are often very sexually aware, and some of them know how to swear with an ease that would make a squaddie blush. Every one of them demands immense emotional commitment and stamina; but they are also intensely rewarding, because I know that a weekend of respite in my home is giving them a break from their own lives.

I hope that not one of them has heard me complain. Even when I'm ready to fall asleep on my feet, I show them a positive, smiling face. Many of them have known nothing but criticism and neglect: a cheerful response can actually feel puzzling to them. They goad me, trying to restore 'normal service' – an outburst of shouting, a tirade of bad language, a stand-up row. They won't get any of those things from me, no matter how hard they try. And when they realise this, the change in the atmosphere is glorious, as if the sun has come out from behind rainclouds.

My training helps me to stay very calm when a teenager

is shouting and screaming. A friend once dropped round when I was going through a nightmare with one girl who was not even in her teens. My visitor was horrified. She couldn't imagine living with that behaviour, and she instinctively wanted me to put a stop to it. But I knew that couldn't be done by letting myself react, by showing how much it upset me.

My friend said, 'Are you going to let her speak to you like that?'

And I just said, 'Yes.'

The girl was looking for a reaction, trying to provoke a big explosion. It proved better to talk to her later on, when she had calmed down. Talking to her while she was shouting, screaming and swearing was not going to get me anywhere. It was more important to withhold attention while she was kicking up a fuss, and then, when the storm had blown itself out, give her praise for calming down and use positive attention as a reward.

Ignore the bad behaviour and praise the good; I've always found it's worked for me. Tell children that they're good and they behave. When you see them happy and you know you've made a difference, and they leave and they want to come back again, it's the best feeling in the world.

I went to a Christmas party last year and met a boy I had fostered for three weeks. He had not been the easiest of young men, and he said, 'Why were you being so nice to me when I was so horrible to you?'

He'd obviously given this some thought during the following months, because he really wanted to know.

I said, 'I really didn't notice. I think you're a smashing

lad.' To give him that confidence and reassurance is more important than anyone can imagine. I know that if I had been through hard times and had low self-esteem, as a lot of these children have, I might react the same way. You can't blame them for having short fuses: violent and abusive behaviour are perhaps all they've ever known. So if you can give them love and a bit of a laugh, you're winning. And I've got a lot of love and laughter to give.

I started to plan for the future. I had no intention of leaving Bridgwater, but to make sure I was prepared for the unexpected, I had registered with an independent fostering agency instead of the local authority. If we move to another part of the country tomorrow, I can take my fostering status with me. Working for an agency means tackling the youngsters with the most challenging problems. Social Services often ask agencies to place the children who won't fit into ordinary foster families.

The agency contacted me one afternoon in 2004 to say they had a little boy with complex medical needs: he was severely epileptic, brain-damaged, couldn't talk or control his movements and, at six years old, was unable to do anything for himself. His mother was devoted to him, but desperately in need of occasional respite. The local authority couldn't find anybody in the area with the nursing skills to care for him. The woman at the agency said, 'We thought you might be the right person to help.'

I said I'd be very interested and so they contacted his mother, Su, who brought her son over to meet me. He stayed with me for the first time about a month after that, and Su bent over backwards to enable me to give him the best care. She is utterly dedicated to her son. We went over everything: how his machines worked, what crises could arise, how he would make his needs known. He has very bad fits and also suffers from serious chest infections. He's a very sick little boy, but he has the most enormous and beautiful blue eyes.

He was born normal, but his epilepsy is so severe that one of his fits left him brain-damaged. He can't talk, but he communicates with sounds and facial expressions. He's quite capable of telling me off if he doesn't like something, such as when he's having his medication.

I have him for four days and nights every month, and would willingly have him for longer, because he's become part of my family. I now have official status in his family, too, because Su has awarded me the title of 'Official Auntie Barbara'. The greatest reward comes from doing activities together, such as a walk under trees in the park when the sun is shining through the branches. He will look up and see the play of light and shade in the leaves, and he'll make a happy noise. When that happens, it's possible to forget everything and share a simple moment of undiluted pleasure.

It was at this time that someone special came into my life. After a year alone I had decided to join a dating agency, and I met David. He was very charming and we hit it off straight away. So, things were good. My finances were stable, the fostering was going well, and the boys were flourishing. I thought that finally we'd achieved stability and a well-earned happy ending.

Chapter Five

It was just like being slapped in the face. To be told I had cancer was the biggest shock of my life. The news hit me so hard it felt like a physical blow.

The toughest fights of my life were surely behind me: I believed that beyond doubt. The idea that something awful had begun to happen was unthinkable.

I'd gone to the doctor in February 2005 because I'd felt a lump under my left arm when showering. I rang the doctor's surgery. A similar lump the previous year had been benign, so this one didn't worry me. I was getting it checked out because ignoring it would be irresponsible; but I was simply going through the motions. It was as if by asking my GP to take a look at it, I was automatically confirming the lump was harmless – a cyst, or something equally trivial.

I knew that nine out of ten lumps are not cancerous, so initially I was not too worried when my doctor said he would fast-track me for hospital tests. The concept of cancer remained wholly abstract. I knew what the tests would be looking for, but cancer remained a disease that 'other people' had. The possibility that I might have a serious illness was something I acknowledged only at the most superficial level.

At Taunton Musgrove Hospital, I underwent a mammogram, in which a machine scans the breast for growths. I am grateful that mine is the first generation that can afford to take these life-saving scanners for granted.

After the mammogram, the technicians did an ultrasound, bombarding the lump with inaudible sounds to gauge its shape by measuring the echoes. One of the nurses slipped me a piece of reassurance: 'We think it's probably a cyst because it's very round. You'll be all right.'

I was now feeling more confident that it would not be cancer. However, the medics decided to do a needle biopsy just to be sure. I had to wait an hour and a half for the results. I had better things to do than sit around: my respite child was going to be staying with us that evening and I had promised Ash I'd take both of them bowling in Weston-super-Mare. If the tests dragged on much longer, I'd be late when I collected Ash from school, late on the M5, which would be thick with commuter traffic, late when we reached Su's house and too late altogether for bowling.

By the end of ninety minutes I had worked myself into a fine state of impatience, and when at last the doctor called me in for the results, I was thoroughly fed up of waiting.

From the moment he gestured for me to sit down, I was talking at him: 'I've got to go and pick up my foster child. I'm very busy and haven't got much time.'

The doctor cleared his throat and started to explain about cell changes. I'm a nurse: I know what cell changes mean. He said I would need an operation, but it still just wasn't registering.

I said, 'Well, if it's got to come out, I don't know where

I'll fit you in, because I'll have to arrange things with the children's hospice,' and I carried on talking.

The doctor sat there and he must have been thinking, Oh my God, she doesn't understand. He looked at me with such compassion and said, 'Barbara, it's cancer.'

With a gasp, I suddenly stopped talking. I could feel the flush rising. The shock hit me. I simply couldn't believe it.

The doctor was kind, and so sympathetic. And I felt such a fool because I should have known from the outset what he was talking about. But I had blocked it out. From the moment I found the lump, my conscious mind had been in denial. I've seen that so many times in patients that it's embarrassing to realise I gave in to the same delusion.

In an effort to take control, I tried to be businesslike: 'Let's get this thing out of my body as quickly as possible. When can I come in?' All those other commitments in my life had instantly taken on a different perspective: my overriding responsibility was to get better as quickly as possible because my children needed me to be well and strong.

The doctor was confident and efficient: 'We'll book you in now,' he said. 'I'll talk to the breast-care nurse. You will need to have an operation, and then radiotherapy and chemotherapy if it has spread.'

And then reality really hit me. I said, 'Oh my God, my babies, my children.' Words cannot describe what I was feeling. When I stood up, my legs were like curls of paper. I was blinded by tears, and I was out of my mind with fear and terror. I walked out, my head buzzing, trying to take in what was happening to me. After five minutes of sitting in my car, staring blindly in disbelief at the windscreen, I turned the key in the ignition and set off to collect Ash. We were in time to go bowling, so I went round to Su's to pick up her son, but I was still in shock and operating on automatic pilot.

Su knew I'd been due in for the mammogram and she said, 'You didn't have to come, you know. Are you OK?'

I didn't want Ash to hear so I whispered to her that I had cancer.

She said, 'Oh my God, Barbara, are you all right to have him?'

'Oh, yes, I'm fine.'

But I wasn't fine. I couldn't absorb it, the shock was terrible. In spite of that, we went bowling as planned. Even though part of my brain had accepted the diagnosis, it was difficult to comprehend and so I busied myself. For the next four days I looked after my foster child. He is very time-consuming and so I didn't get much sleep: I had to give him oxygen, clear his lungs and throat by suction, and keep him clean, as well as giving him love and care. I was grateful for the distraction. But when he went home, the devastating truth hit me.

I had cancer. I was very ill, possibly dying. The thought of it was shattering, and my courage left me. I didn't tell Ash, but I broke the news to Richard. In the mornings and evenings, I was functioning enough to look after Ash, but while he was at school I sat on the sofa and stared at the wall. I didn't even have the will to turn on the television. For two weeks I was paralysed with shock, awaiting the operation.

Richard couldn't believe the news. 'Oh, Mum,' he said,

'you are so young. I can't take it in.' I kept my worst fears from Ash and didn't let him see me when I was really down. I'd wash my face, brush my hair, shake myself and try to find a smile to wear before I saw either of my boys. But Richard knew I was ill and he needed to be comforted. I had to be strong for him, even though I didn't feel well enough to be strong for myself.

To make matters worse, David, my boyfriend at the time, was not coping. Not everyone can deal with the emotional strain when someone close to them is ill, and I felt he fell into that category. I was so worried about him that I rang up his sister-in-law to ask her to be there for him, as he couldn't talk to me about the cancer.

When the time came, I went in for the operation. My friend Gina dropped me off because David was working. He visited me in the evening, but we both found it awkward to talk.

As the first stage of my treatment, I needed a lumpectomy on both sides. Pre-cancerous tissue had been found in my other breast during an MRI scan: the image showed up a suspicious area in the right breast, so I had tissue removed from both of them.

The children's hospice was wonderful. They took Ash when I went into hospital. Meanwhile one of the things I had to do was to make my will. I was concerned that Ash would go back into the care system, as his blood relatives were unable to look after him. I thought, Who would love him as much as me?

My brother Paul, who had obviously thought long and hard about this, said, 'I will be there for you and Ash. If the worst happens, we'll take him into our family.' And Robert said to me, 'I brought him up and if you want me to have him, I will. I've thought it through and I'm prepared to do that.'

So I had support from two men who were absolutely wonderful. Neither of them was in a position to easily take on such a responsibility, which made their kindness and their sacrifice all the more touching, especially as, at the time, the thought that my will might be needed was very real indeed.

What moved me most was Richard. He came forward and said, 'Mum, I would never let Ash go into care. I would take him on. He's my brother and I would never, ever let him go into some place where nobody loved him.'

He was eighteen. I thought, What a man I've raised.

He meant what he said. He'd thought it through and for an eighteen-year-old that is nothing short of astonishing.

Ash used to have a social worker who had done the same for her little sister when her parents were killed. She was about twenty-three and she had an eight-year-old sister living with her. She told me, 'It was very hard when I was nineteen to take her on.' I remembered that and it made me appreciate Richard even more. My son was brilliant, absolutely brilliant.

But I was a dreadful patient. I was frightened about going into the operating theatre because I thought I might not wake up from the anaesthetic. Nurses are the worst worriers when it comes to operations.

After the operation, I thought I would never feel the same again. I was sure I'd think about cancer every single day of my life – having scarcely thought of it at all before. It had become so all-consuming, I couldn't fix my mind on anything else. Of course, nowadays I think of other things all the time. My life isn't about cancer at all now; it's about staying well, getting on with life and appreciating it. But during that initial period, it was an obsession.

Perhaps people will think I was silly to worry about something as trivial as my looks when my life was on the line, but after the lumpectomy I didn't want to look at myself in the mirror. I had had a good cosmetic result, or at least that's what the doctors tell me, but I couldn't move very well – because I'd had lymph nodes removed from under my arms – and was very sore.

Gina brought me home after the surgery. It was a beautiful day and I noticed the sun. Suddenly my mood lifted. I thought, What a lovely day. I'm looking at the flowers, I'm noticing the smells, and I'm feeling the warmth of the sun. That awareness has never left me. I notice things so much more.

My brother Paul came to look after me, He managed just a couple of days and then he left. He had tears in his eyes when he went. He said, 'I can't do this.' He was so upset, yet it wasn't as if I was depressed or crying, because by this point I was feeling more cheerful. I was relieved the cancer had been cut out. He found being with me very stressful: I think when you start coping, other people fall apart.

I think all women worry about feeling and looking unfeminine, and I was no exception. I was hoping that David would say my scar didn't matter, but he wouldn't even look at it and that made me feel terrible. It was a friend of Su's who has taken on the role of her son's surrogate grandfather who made me smile. He's got a really cheeky sense of humour. I was fretting that I was going to be flat-chested, and instead of telling me I was talking nonsense, he said, 'Never mind, Barbara, you've still got the best bum in the south-west of England.' Totally the wrong thing to say, but it made me laugh anyway.

After the operation, the doctor explained that I would need a course of radiotherapy. I was fine with that: I was just happy that the cancer had gone. I was determined not to face the next consultation alone. One month later, I went along to the consultation with my ex, Robert, who has been a pillar of strength at every step of my fight. The Disneyland Paris episode was in the past, we were no longer partners, and he was in a new relationship. We had something more important: we were friends. And I was desperately grateful for his support.

I was hoping against hope that the specialist would say, 'We've removed all the cancer. Have some radiotherapy and then you'll be fine.' I knew the overall survival rate for cancer was 85 per cent. But the consultant started saying that my cancer was 'very aggressive' and I knew my fight wasn't over; it was only just beginning.

A couple of weeks before my appointment, I had rung the hospital because I wanted to know the results. I had tricked the nurse with my confidence: 'It's all right, I'm a nurse myself and I've worked in this field. I know all about it, nothing's going to shock me, you can tell me – what are my results?'

I was actually interested in whether the cancer was

oestrogen-receptive or not, because that would affect the types of treatment available to me. She looked through my notes and said, 'That's good – it is oestrogen-receptive. It ought to respond to hormone therapy. But, oh dear . . . you're HER2 positive and you're a low PS2. But never mind, at least it's oestrogen-receptive.'

'Oh, yes,' I said, 'that's good!' And then of course I went straight on to the Internet to find out what all that meant!

It wasn't just that HER2 was one of the most deadly cancers around; what made it worse, as bad as it could be, was the low PS2. That's a predictive score. Low PS2 corresponded to 'high risk of recurrence and early death'. I rang the hospital in a state of distress and demanded an immediate appointment. Their response was excellent and I was seen by a doctor two days later – they were no doubt aware they'd given me the results over the phone and I hadn't coped well, even though I'd wheedled them out. This consultation would help me find out what the results really meant.

The doctor said, 'It's a very serious, very aggressive cancer, and when the surgeons removed it they got a very narrow margin.' In other words, virtually none of the tissue had been cut out beyond the cancer on one side. She continued, 'So we'll give you a boost of five weeks' radiotherapy instead of four, but you will need chemotherapy because we have found cancer in your lymph nodes.'

That was a shock. I'd been expecting radiotherapy but not chemotherapy, which can make patients feel very ill.

The doctor pulled no punches: 'You will have a year out of your life with treatment. You will lose your hair, but it will grow back beautifully.'

I said, 'What are my chances of survival? What are my odds?'

She said, 'I don't think it's helpful for you to know that.' She might as well have said, 'Abandon all hope.'

I said, 'I really want to know.'

'Well, with chemotherapy it's fourteen per cent.'

Robert and I exchanged glances, and we both thought it was a death sentence.

Robert asked, 'Is there any advantage to her going privately?'

'I'll find out if a consultant in Bristol can see you,' she replied.

Robert and I walked out, and we both thought that was it. It was a devastating consultation.

Chapter Six

I don't know which sounds worse: your chances of survival are just 14 per cent, or there's an 86 per cent probability that this cancer will kill you. Either way, it's not the news you want to hear.

My instinct is to fight. As long as I'm breathing, I've got hope. But for several weeks I was so down there didn't seem to be any way back up again. I felt like giving up. And then I forced myself to focus on that narrow escape route.

Put a hundred women with that type of breast cancer in a room and fourteen will walk out alive, that's what the statistics said. And I couldn't allow myself to be left in that room to die. Ash needed me. He was my responsibility. I could simply not give up, not when there was a hope of being one of the fourteen who could cheat death.

But how could I win a place in that minority?

At this stage, I wasn't remotely thinking about saving the rest of the women in that room. The realisation came later that even one in a hundred was too high a mortality rate, never mind eighty-six. To start with, I was focused only on my own chances. That's what the survival instinct is about.

I started on an extreme vegan diet, though it only lasted three days. The reaction of many people when the diagnosis is cancer is to try something drastic like that. At any support group, you'll hear as much about diets as about treatments, and I was as desperate as anyone. I changed my toothpaste, I changed my deodorant. There was no indication of what had caused my cancer, and I was ready to blame anything. I drink in moderation, I don't smoke, I'm slim, and I was at a loss to know where the disease had come from. I don't fit any of the typical profiles. Breast cancer doesn't run in my family.

I tried all the things the books recommend, including physical exercise, but it felt hopeless. If changing your toothpaste and doing sit-ups was a guarantee of good health, we'd all be doing it. The awful truth is that you can live by the rules – eating well and avoiding tobacco, drinking in moderation and going for long strolls in the fresh country air – and you might still get cancer.

I kept asking my friends, 'How can I make sure I'm one of the fourteen in a hundred? If I knew, I'd do it.' But nobody could tell me. After all, there's no way of saying you haven't simply inherited the genetic short straw. I really did start to think, This is it. My number's come up and I'm going to die.

And then I thought of my doctor's words, about losing a year of my life. She wasn't trying to buck me up; she was simply warning me of what lay ahead. But it galvanised me: she'd said, 'You will have a year out of your life with treatment.'

I thought, A year out of my life? My God! If the rest of my life is going to be short, I'm not consenting to having a year taken out of it.

I got up off my deathbed and I decided to live. I dragged

myself into the shower, put on my make-up and vowed I'd face the world every day.

When I went to see the private consultant, Dr Hassan, he had squeezed me in for the last appointment, at around 8.30 p.m. He greeted me with such a warm smile that I immediately started to feel a little better. The appointment lasted for more than an hour. He didn't try to hurry it – it was as if he had all the time in the world for me. During the course of a long chat, he gave me better odds of survival and a great deal of information and explanations I hadn't had before. I was grateful, for he really sat down and explained my situation to me in detail.

We discussed how my cancer was a particularly deadly variety, HER2 positive. Instead of focusing on the bleak prognosis, he looked at the overall survival rates with breast cancer and cheered me up by lifting my confidence. The first step to beating cancer is in the mind – I needed to believe I had a fighting chance, and Dr Hassan gave me that.

He also said, 'There's a drug called Herceptin. It's being used on people with the later stages of HER2-positive breast cancer with great success. It can keep people alive for some years longer. If your cancer comes back, you can expect to get this drug on the NHS, but at this early stage it won't be prescribed to you. We suspect Herceptin might also be helpful to early-stage sufferers, but the results of the trials are not available yet. The interim trial results are looking very positive, but it is likely to be a long time before the drug is available on the NHS for women like you.

'Unfortunately, because you're not covered by medical

insurance, you're unlikely to be able to afford this drug even if the trial results are good. Quite frankly, the cost would be astronomical. But your overall prognosis is looking good, so forget I mentioned Herceptin – you don't really need it.

'Please don't be frightened of having cancer. Try to think of it as a chronic illness, and that you might have bouts of cancer throughout your lifetime. We have tremendous success with keeping people alive for many years now.'

That made a great impact on me. Thinking of it as a long-term illness is a huge help. I felt bolstered for a couple of days – and then I went on the Internet and looked again at the figures, and my heart sank into the pit of my stomach.

My original consultant, Dr Bryant, had been right all along. There was an 86 per cent probability that I wouldn't survive this cancer. More optimistic assessments had not taken account of my PS2, the low predictive score and had ignored the tests that revealed the growth had been HER2 positive.

That knocked the stuffing out of me. I sat down and for the rest of April I waited to die.

Then I started on my chemo, and that's when I experienced what death is like. But before the drugs could even start to work, there was another blow to come.

On the first day of my chemo, I was due into hospital at 2 p.m. I had already told my fostering agency that I was having treatment for cancer, though I was worried that they would not allow me to keep working.

It is not in my nature to hide things: if my hair was going to fall out, people were going to notice – I wouldn't try to pretend to my social worker that I'd done a sponsored head-shave. So I had resolved to be honest and upfront from the start, and had told my social worker all the facts.

I was keen to continue fostering my respite child, as I had become very fond of him and close to Su. I said that I realised I would not be able to manage other children, particularly those with challenging behavioural problems, but I really wanted to continue looking after Su's little boy. Su herself had been brilliant, arriving regularly with her Red Cross parcels full of health foods such as bean sprouts and soya products. She was quite determined to make sure I stayed well.

We had all thought that chemo would be unnecessary and on that basis I had continued to foster after my operation. With the news that I would have to start chemotherapy, the agency had to hand the decision about whether I could continue over to a panel. My social worker's timing was bad: she rang on the morning of my first chemo. I was already upset when the social worker called, and nothing could be harder than a phone conversation to say I might be unemployable.

Although the agency was acting entirely within the law and actually had to do this, I still felt victimised. It was keeping busy that gave me strength, and to have that possibility taken away, on a day when I was more scared than I had ever been in my life, was unbearable.

When I arrived at the oncology unit, my doctor could see I was distressed and she said, 'I'll write to the panel and explain your treatment in detail. I'll point out that other people manage to work through chemo, and as long as you are sensible about the times you care for this child, I'm sure there will be no problem.'

That was a good point: you are not automatically signed off work when you have a cancer diagnosis, and for many people work is the lifeline that pulls them through.

My case went before the panel a couple of weeks later. I stated my arguments for continuing to foster in a letter. As she had promised, my doctor also supplied a letter to explain what my treatment involved, Su wrote in support as well, saying she had absolute faith in me, and even my social worker argued on my behalf. I had to make it plain that I was not in denial, that I fully understood I was going to have chemotherapy and was not trying to minimise the seriousness of my treatment.

The upshot was that the panel approved me to look after Su's son throughout my chemotherapy, but I could not foster any other children, which was fine. I also had to be careful about dates, as I was not allowed to have him on chemotherapy days or for several days afterwards: I simply would not be well enough to care for him.

Su was keen to help with this and, true to her word, supported me by fitting in with my chemotherapy dates and staying on call at all times, in case I got ill.

In the midst of all this, I still had to take care of Ash. Until this point, I had said as little as possible to him. A mother's duty is to protect her children, not burden them with worries. When I went into hospital, I explained it away airily: 'Mummy had a little lump removed, that's all. It's fine.' And naturally, being eleven, he took my words at face value.

When it became clear I would have to go through chemotherapy, I realised I had to tell Ash that it wasn't 'fine'. I delayed the news for as long as I could, but then one of my friend's children overheard a discussion about my illness. There was a risk Ash would hear about it in the playground. So I told him that my lump wasn't a good lump, that it was something called a cancer. It had been all removed, but my doctors felt it was better to be safe than sorry, so I was going to have some medicine that would make me very sick. I had to get sick before I got better, and there would be days when I wasn't very well. I would probably lose my hair, though he wasn't to worry because it would grow back.

Telling Ash was one of the hardest things I have done in my life. If there had been any way to protect him, I would have seized it. But he absorbed the news calmly. For a child of eleven, he had extraordinary reserves of bravery. He simply said, 'I don't want you to be ill.'

I waved him off to his Saturday club, and as I watched him go, I knew he would be worried sick inside. He had lost his own mother, and the shock of realising he might lose me too must have been incredibly difficult for him. I had tried to keep the news low-key, but even an eleven-year-old knows what cancer is.

I later heard that he cried all the way through Saturday club. I felt so guilty. It's ridiculous that anyone could feel guilty with cancer, but I did: I had taken on a poorly child, pledging to nurse him and taking my own health for granted, and now I didn't know whether I'd be able to fulfil my responsibility to him. I couldn't even promise him that

I would always be there. It felt as if I was giving him a worse life, forcing him to go through more worry and the fear of more loss. He had done nothing to deserve such a raw deal, and although I couldn't have done anything to avoid cancer, the guilt was terrible.

To allay his worst fears, we talked about the cancer treatment freely, and I kept the tone cheerful and upbeat. Richard would come round and Ash would be very cuddly and clingy with us, but otherwise he didn't show any obvious distress. His social worker arranged for him to have extra support from the Saturday-club staff, who proved extremely helpful in guiding him through his feelings.

Ash stayed at the local children's hospice when I went into hospital. The administrator carried on offering this service during my worst chemo weeks.

How bad those weeks were, I could never have imagined.

Chapter Seven

Chemotherapy is sometimes misunderstood. It actually just means treatment with chemicals. When you have cancer, you are treated with cytotoxic drugs, a cocktail of poisonous toxins, which kill cells that are actively growing and dividing, so although the chemotherapy kills the cancer, parts of your body's healthy cells that divide frequently are likely to be affected too, leading to some severe side effects. However, chemotherapy does increase the survival rates for breast cancer, and reduces the chances of it returning.

The drugs are injected into a vein over several hours every three to four weeks. A complete course can take between six and eight months. Side effects can affect your mouth, digestive system, skin, hair and bone marrow, leading to a suppressed immune system.

A friend who had already been through chemotherapy advised me to just have a light breakfast treatment days. She also suggested that I carried some boiled sweets to help disguise the metallic aftertaste of the drug once it had been injected.

My friend Gina took me to the hospital and insisted on staying with me during the treatment. The nurse brought over a syringe filled with a bright-red drug, which she explained was the chemotherapy. She set up a drip and gave me some anti-sickness medication through the line, before putting on purple gloves and protective goggles and administering the drug. I was so afraid because I didn't know what lay ahead.

The treatment took three and a half hours to administer. I felt OK while having it. Immediately afterwards I felt a little shaky, but it was not too bad and I was fine to walk out of the hospital. I had made arrangements for Ash to stay overnight with Gina, and for Richard to come round and look after me.

At this point, I thought I was going to be all right with the treatment. I rang my mother and said I was feeling fine. But at about 7 p.m. the effects hit me. I started to feel as if I had flu and so went to bed. I could not have envisaged how bad it would get.

That first session of chemotherapy is burned into my memory like a scar. It's unpleasant and embarrassing to recall, but I feel strongly that it's only worth telling my story if I'm completely honest and leave nothing out.

Later that evening, as the poison took hold, I started to vomit. I found myself half lying, half hanging on to the rim of the toilet bowl, shaking like a heroin addict. It was so severe that I had vomit over my face, and the retching caused me to wet myself. I had diarrhoea, which I was unable to control. I thought I was dying. That's how bad it can be. Within days my mouth was covered with ulcers, I was constantly sick, and still had diarrhoea. I had to return to the hospital, where I told my doctor how ill I felt. A blood test revealed that my immune system had been severely affected by the medication. From this point she reduced the drugs by 10 per cent and it was never as bad after that.

That was my own experience, and every patient is different. Once I'd had the first dose, I knew I was over the worst, and it certainly helped that my doctor was able to reduce the strength of the infusion. Even so, the degradation and horror of my situation appalled me, and all I could think was, This is the low point of my life. This is what cancer has done to me.

To be hanging with both hands on to the edge of the toilet, shaking, so ill I couldn't even clean myself up – I was horrified that I could have come to this. It didn't seem possible to be so degraded and still be alive.

I have since spoken to lots of people who haven't been so badly affected. I had a friend who used to go and get a takeaway afterwards – how, I don't know. My friend and fellow campaigner Jayne Sullivan took it very well, until she had to be admitted to hospital with a chest infection, which could have led to serious complications. Fortunately, I didn't need to be admitted to hospital; instead, I felt rough the whole way through.

Before cancer I had been healthy: I was fit and I ate well. I walked the dog for miles. I was slim, and it's scarcely an exaggeration to say I was at the peak of fitness: I did North African dance, for instance, an easy-going style of dancing that appealed to me because Ash's mother came from that part of the world.

What made my diagnosis hard to deal with was how suddenly cancer affected my life, the shock of having my body and my whole world turned inside out. Two months earlier, there hadn't been anything wrong with me, as far as I knew, and I'd felt so well. I was forty-nine years old. I couldn't believe this had happened to me.

I had no predisposing factors at all, apart from the stresses I'd faced during the past few years; but they were all in the past. How could they be inflicting this fresh misery on me in the present? The injustice of it created a lot of anger and confusion inside me.

Gradually I realised, I can't solve this problem. What I can solve is my attitude towards it. I was talking to a male friend the other day, who claimed, 'All problems can be solved.'

And I said, 'That's not true. We can't solve Ash's health problems, for instance. But we can solve the way we look at them, by looking through different eyes. You can't make other people deal with it differently, but you can make your own attitude towards other people more understanding.'

You can't change all your problems. Sometimes you inherit them. I couldn't change the fact that I had cancer: I had no control over that. Nothing is worse than losing control, but you can identify the things you can control and use that knowledge. You have to take a grip on your attitude, and say, 'I can get up every morning and I can face the world.'

With that attitude I survived my first dose of chemotherapy. After that it was never quite as bad. Chemo can cause lethal complications, and there is no doubt that at times I thought I was dying. Even death wouldn't have felt that bad. It was like a combination of gastric flu and coming off heroin – I've only seen heroin withdrawal in television dramas, but when the addicts shake and vomit, that's what my treatment felt like.

I've never felt that ill in my entire life. I've had flu, I've had operations, but I have never felt remotely as ill as that. But I survived. Feeling dreadful, I lay in bed for a few days, staring at the wall, thinking my life was over, and then I thought, Blow this! I either lie here or I get myself in that shower. So I did. I got up, hanging on to the furniture, and forced myself across the room.

There were no other adults around, no one looking after me – just Richard and Ash. Richard was living just down the road at the time, but he came round the first night of my chemo. He even moved back in for a couple of months because I was so poorly. Many young men would have run away, but he had too much courage for that.

Richard did what he could, but no mother wants her sons to see her in that state. I could have done with a full-time nurse, but I had to make do with nursing myself. At least I had plenty of experience of dealing with the sick, even if I wasn't used to playing patient and matron at the same time. It must be a nightmare to fall ill and have to look after yourself if you haven't got any idea what to do.

While I was confined to bed and bathroom, Richard was looking after Ash. On more than one occasion when I'd had chemotherapy, Ash slipped out of the house and hid for hours at a time. He couldn't cope with seeing me in such distress. My neighbours would help find him because I couldn't walk. I couldn't even drag myself out of the house. One night I had to call out the police to find him. While they were hunting for him, he would be hiding in the trees behind our house. It was terrifying.

Chemotherapy had many side effects I couldn't have

imagined, and the effect on Ash was just one of them. Others were simply physical, but they had distressing psychological implications: my vision was affected and my hearing became poor. Both those developments were frightening and upsetting. The doctors assured me my sight would return, but it didn't happen immediately.

I also had terrible word blindness. I couldn't remember basic words like wardrobe: I'd be saying, 'You know, the big wooden boxy thing you put your clothes in.' I can laugh about it now, but at the time it was embarrassing and frustrating.

Other people have told me that their vision, their hearing, their minds were affected by chemotherapy, but the doctors hadn't warned me about these things. I believe doctors need to be more open – for example, I should have been told about how sore your bottom would be. I know that's too much information, but I suffered such bad diarrhoea I couldn't even sit down. I was so raw I didn't know what to do with myself.

On my next visit to the doctor's, I steeled myself to explain how sore I was, and she said, 'Ah! Chemotherapy bottom!' Apparently it was quite common, and wholly normal. That information was reassuring, but I should have been given it much sooner.

That's what's nice about cancer support groups: you can talk about anything. You can talk about losing all your body hair, but nobody discusses that outside a support group. A friend of mine says she looks like a newborn rat because she's lost her hair everywhere. I told her, 'Look on the bright side: it's great that you don't have to shave your legs or pluck your eyebrows.'

Losing my hair was one of the worst aspects of the entire experience. It hurts when it comes out. I noticed at first that it had gone very flat, and then when I went out and the wind blew, it was like someone was tugging at my scalp. It hurts because you don't lose one or two hairs at a time – you lose it all together. The doctors didn't warn me about that either. I wish I had been offered a cold cap, which freezes your head during chemo and sometimes allows you to keep your hair.

I cut my hair very short, with clippers, down to a number two and then a number one, until it was the texture of suede. But it was still falling out in clumps. Wherever I went I was moulting, leaving handfuls of hair. I looked like a gorilla in the shower, as it plastered itself to my arms and shoulders. I would never have believed I had so much hair on my head.

That went on for about three days, and I thought, I've got to cut it all off. So I went in the bathroom and completely shaved my scalp. I filled the bowl with tears and hair.

I came out of the bathroom and Ash was sitting on the stairs. Quietly, he started to cry.

I said, 'Whatever's the matter?'

He said, 'I can't cope with all this stress.'

I pulled myself together instantly. One moment I was sobbing and sniffing, the next I was coping. It was an instinctive reaction: my child needed to be protected from the emotional strain, and the only person who could do that was me.

There are benefits to be drawn from any experience, no matter how negative, and my illness did bring one unexpected bonus, which emerged slowly. Ash has been in and out of hospital all his life: it's part of his subconscious self-image. He's 'the poorly one'. That's not how he wants to see himself, but illness has been a huge part of his life. And suddenly I was the one at death's door.

His reaction was, in effect, 'What about me? I'm the most important person in this family. I'm the ill one. How dare you be ill? I can't have this!'

In a strange way, my illness has done him the world of good. He's come on in leaps and bounds, and he's now a normal child. He's no longer 'the ill one'. He's learned that he can't see himself as a victim – life is more complicated than that.

And I refuse to be a victim. I will not be. Call me a 'cancer victim' and I'll call you something straight back. My refusal to be a victim began when I emerged from the bathroom bald as a hard-boiled egg. I forced a smile on my face and decided to get on with living.

I hadn't thought about the chill factor, though, and with no hair at all, my head was cold. It wasn't just cold; it was also prickly, which hurt and itched. At first I thought I couldn't do much more than keep it warm, so I borrowed a woolly hat from Ash. I went round for the rest of the day in an Exeter City football hat – let's just say it wasn't my best look. The question of what to wear when I had no hair had never crossed my mind. Nor had I realised quite how different I would look. I'd never seen my scalp properly before, the dips and scrapes, the little scars – I've got a scar at the back where I struck my head on a garage door. No one had ever seen it before, least of all me.

I looked a mess, wearing this woolly hat. A doctor friend of mine came round and sympathised. The next morning she delivered a consignment of headscarves to my door.

They were brilliant. I discovered myself. I discovered I was a style icon. From that point on I wore headscarves and did the rounds of the charity shops, bulk-buying them.

I'd tie a headscarf round this way, and then I'd roll another one and tie it round the other way, and then I'd tie a big bow on top or at the back. There are a lot of charity shops in Bridgwater, all of which sell headscarves . . . and I now own most of them!

When I eventually started going on television, women were ringing me up from as far away as Edinburgh, asking, 'Where do you buy your headscarves? How do you tie them?' Bristol Cancer Centre got in touch with me to ask if I'd go and teach them some tricks with knots, rolls and twists. I have a potential new career as a Hermès rep – if they can afford me!

Despite my brave face, the cocktail of poisons in my blood often left me doubled over. Some women go through chemotherapy without being sick, and the doctors assured me at the outset that I was unlikely to be physically sick. They can't prevent patients from feeling nauseous, but they claim they can control the vomiting.

But at the end of the treatment, my doctor said, 'We never did get on top of that sickness, did we?'

The last time I had chemotherapy, I had to call a doctor to my home to give me an injection to prevent me from vomiting. I couldn't cope with it any more. Much of the reaction was psychological, a Pavlovian reaction – I used to be sick as soon as I saw the chemotherapy syringe. Eventually, they brought the syringe out covered with a towel and kept it under the towel as they administered it.

Some months later, after I went public with my fight, I had a letter out of the blue from a hypnotherapist named Andrew. He said he very much admired the way I was coping with things and he could teach me some relaxation techniques that might help with the sickness and nausea. Would I like a free session?

I'd never been hypnotised and it sounded fun, as well as relaxing. So I rang Andrew up, thanked him, accepted the offer and along I went for my free session. I'm the kind of person who goes on the dodgems and gets travel sick. I just seem to suffer from nausea more than most people, I wasn't too sure whether hypnosis would work, but I was willing to try. In fact, it didn't cure the problem, but it did change my attitude: I became much more relaxed about my nausea. More importantly, I've gained a friend who has helped a lot over the past few months. Andrew's got a background in general and psychiatric nursing, and I've been able to ring him up and tell him how I'm feeling. He's a very good listener.

A lot of people don't want to hear about the worst aspects of cancer. They especially don't want to talk about death. They want to hear you say, 'I'm coping, I'll be fine,' and then they'll tell their friends how brave you're being.

Actually, it's not about me being brave; it's about whether they are afraid to talk about death.

Andrew has supported me. Most people can't bear to imagine how the world would cope without them, and that's why so few of us make a will or take out life insurance until we can't put it off any longer.

But Andrew said to me, 'If you ever want to talk, you can always call me.' And I have done. Finding someone you can open up to is one of the hardest things, and also one of the most essential.

Andrew helped me to understand more about the way I think. Some people follow their thoughts along straight lines; mine travel in three dimensions. I have an idea and it fires off all over the place.

During my treatment, that was the one thing that was left to me, that I could still do: I could think. My memory was wrecked, but my creativity was intact. Chemotherapy damages the brain and makes it very hard to concentrate. The effect must be shattering for someone who thinks in a methodical, linear way. To lose that ability must feel like madness.

When you're trying to find the handful of facts that could save your life, and you're surrounded by dozens of friends offering helpful advice, hundreds of medical reports and journals, thousands of newspaper stories, hundreds of thousands of websites, a grasshopper brain is a natural advantage. I was able to leap from one idea to another without getting confused, picking up information from a kaleidoscope of sources.

That, coupled with my sheer determination, saved my life.

Chapter Eight

Uri Geller had been phoning Ash every month for years to hear how he was doing with his lessons and his karate. My junior superstar was unfazed by the calls from his famous friend – if Justin Timberlake called to invite him to dance in his next video, Ash would be delighted but not surprised. He has blossomed into a charismatic and confident youngster, with a stream of friends who are constantly calling round to our home.

I was used to Uri calling the house, but I was touched and grateful after my diagnosis when he started to call me regularly, as well as Ash. Many people don't know how to react when an acquaintance develops cancer. They don't know what to say, so they stop saying anything.

Uri was different. When I told him I had breast cancer, he stepped up his calls and contacted us every week, to give pep talks and pass on rumours about that week's miracle cure. I'm amazed that he has the time, and his energy is inspirational. After a ten-minute bombardment of intense positive-thinking mantras, I feel regenerated. Attitude counts for an enormous amount in any fight for health, and Uri knows how to grab my attitude by the scruff of its neck and haul it upwards. He has told me hundreds of times to believe in myself, and at moments when my battle has been toughest, I have focused on those simple, passionate words: 'Barbara, believe in yourself. You can do anything! Have that belief!'

He had also called more than once to recommend alternative therapies – Uri's belief is that I should make the maximum use of conventional medicines, and never abandon them, but use the alternatives where they seem appropriate. That's how I feel, too: complementary medicine, such as hypnotherapy, is worth investigating, but if you want to stay alive you have to use doctors, hospitals and properly trialled drugs.

One evening at the end of April 2005, at about 7 p.m., Uri rang. I was feeling weak and low, and it was as much as I could do to reach for the phone.

'Barbara! You have to go out right this minute and buy the *Daily Telegraph*,' he commanded.

'I'm feeling pretty grim tonight, Uri. Can't it wait till tomorrow?' I pleaded.

In the months since my diagnosis I had read thousands of column inches in the national newspapers and on the Internet, and so much of what appeared at first to hold out hope was over-hyped or under-researched. I was fairly certain that whatever Uri had read would turn out to be a couple of dubious paragraphs about evening primrose oil or the benefits of organic mangoes.

Uri was adamant: 'You have to go out and get it, you have to. NOW!' There's no arguing with him. He might not have a medical background, but when it comes to health matters he is unstoppable.

I thought, Oh, blow it. I put my shoes on, got in the car

and drove down the road to the newsagent's. Fortunately, it was a short journey – perhaps if I'd had to trek to the supermarket, I would not have had the energy. The smallest factors can have the greatest significance in any fight – that's why I always urge myself to make the extra effort, even when it seems futile.

I've always said that Uri Geller saved my life with that phone call.

I bought the *Telegraph*, took it home, opened it at the page Uri had told me to read, and saw a piece about Herceptin. The name was vaguely familiar, from my discussion with Dr Hassan, but I had read nothing about it in the press. I later learned the *Telegraph* had picked up an exclusive: this was the very first article about the drug, on the day of the release of the dramatic trial results by the manufacturer of Herceptin, Roche.

The story was by the paper's health correspondent, Nic Fleming, and it kicked off with a startling statistic: Herceptin, which was used at that time only in the *advanced* stages of breast cancer, had been shown to halve the disease's risk of progressing during the *early* stages. Among patients with the aggressive HER2-positive variety, Herceptin – the brand name for Trastuzumab – slashed the risk of a relapse by more than 50 per cent.

Between a fifth and a quarter of all breast-cancer sufferers have the HER2-positive strain, which is 250 per cent more likely to return after remission than other types of the disease.

My cancer had been HER2 positive. I didn't want to rush to conclusions, but, assuming this report was right,

Herceptin could halve my own chances of suffering a recurrence. I was in the highest-risk group, but these results could reverse the odds. If Herceptin was the wonder drug that early reports suggested, and if my doctors could prescribe a course of it for me, it might help save me.

The item quoted Dr Andrew Wardley, consultant medical oncologist at the Christie Hospital, which is a specialist cancer-treatment centre in Manchester: 'These are outstanding results that offer new hope for women with this aggressive and often fatal form of breast cancer. The use of Herceptin, in addition to chemotherapy post-surgery, could save thousands of lives. It will soon be imperative to determine the HER2 status of all breast-cancer patients at diagnosis to determine who could benefit from such treatment. The NHS needs to make immediate provision for this.'

I had never heard a doctor speak with such excitement and certainty. Usually they are so anxious to protect themselves from future critics all you can hear are 'if's and 'but's. And yet here was a highly respected oncologist virtually jumping up and down with excitement.

I read the story over and over, taking in every detail. One thought grew steadily in my mind: This is probably my only hope of remaining cancer-free. I've been told that if my disease progresses to late-stage breast cancer, Herceptin could keep me alive, possibly for years. But these new trials indicate something altogether different: a course of Herceptin *now* will hugely reduce my chances of developing late-stage breast cancer. This is the key that could unlock my cell door. It is my big hope.

Nic Fleming's reporting seemed authoritative. I knew it

was dangerous to believe everything I read – there are so many conflicting Internet sites and news stories – but as far as I could tell, the *Telegraph* was getting its facts right.

In Britain, the paper said, 5,500 women a year die from HER2 breast cancer. HER2 itself was a protein found on the surface of the cancer cells. The protein molecules acted as 'growth receptors' or connectors: Herceptin blocked the connections. If the results of the trials were repeated in the real world, Herceptin could save 2,800 lives annually in the UK alone.

Those trials looked reliable: they were funded by the US National Cancer Institute and involved 3,300 Americans with early HER2-positive breast cancer. The test patients were split into two groups: a control group who were treated only with chemotherapy and a test group who had chemo and Trastuzumab.

Armed with this information, I rang my private consultant, Dr Hassan, the following morning. The last time I had spoken to him, he had suggested I should go on to a medicine called Arimidex once I finished chemotherapy, because it was the most effective of the new anti-oestrogen drugs. Arimidex was licensed but was not approved by NICE, the National Institute for Health and Clinical Excellence, he had warned. Because it hadn't been approved by NICE, it would not be available on the NHS. So I would have to fight for the treatment. 'You should try to get it,' he had urged, 'because it could increase life expectancy by a few per cent.'

A few per cent? The newspaper report suggested Herceptin would increase chances of survival by 50 per cent or more.

Inevitably, Dr Hassan wasn't available – he was in Miami at the Roche trials, listening to the reports. The news was out, but he hadn't flown home yet and wouldn't be back at his clinic until the end of May – that was four weeks away.

I spoke to his secretary: 'I've seen the results. I want this drug. No matter how much it costs, I want it. I'm going to get it somehow. Even if it means going to America.'

That was my first thought. I knew Herceptin was already available in Canada and the US for early-stage sufferers because I had been Googling all over the Internet to find every scrap of information I could.

As soon as Dr Hassan returned to the country, he rang me. 'You're absolutely right, the results are astounding. This is a wonder drug. But I have to warn you that it is exceptionally expensive and it will not immediately become available on the NHS to you. There's no doubt that the trials are exceptional, and NICE will have to consider it for licensing and approval. But that could take years, and without their go-ahead, the NHS won't prescribe it to you.'

I understood what he was saying: the NHS is a bureau-cracy. Patients are all individuals, all unique human beings, but the NHS has to operate as if we were minute parts in an immense machine. The bureaucracy would not consider prescribing Herceptin to one individual: it would make the drug available to all, or none. And if some of the tiny parts were lost in the giant cogs, that was how the machine worked.

But I knew there were alternatives. The NHS was not the only way to obtain healthcare. It was the method I most believed in, the system that I'd devoted most of my working life to helping; but in a fight for my life, I wouldn't hesitate to try other methods. I certainly would not sit for years with my fingers crossed, waiting for NICE to grant a licence and approve the drug. If I did, Herceptin might be saving thousands of women from early-stage breast cancer in a decade's time, but I wouldn't be alive to see it.

'You say it's going to be exceptionally expensive – how expensive?' I demanded.

That's when I heard the first tentative figure: 'I think it's probably going to be in the region of £50,000 for the first year,' Dr Hassan said. 'And ideally you'll have it for two years, though I think even if you could take it for six months it might work.'

This was just days after the trials were first reported, and Dr Hassan's estimate was a brave one. He was erring on the side of caution, but I was grateful for that: it was better than having my hopes raised with a low estimate. It was more than I had imagined a drug could possibly cost, and far more than I could borrow at the bank; yet I knew I would get it somehow. I'd have to, if the alternative was death.

'Surely you couldn't afford it,' he said.

'I'll raise the money,' I retorted. 'I've got my house. I can sell it.'

The doctor was horrified. 'You can't sell your house to buy a drug.'

I said, 'Well, there's no pockets in a shroud. It's very little use to me dead. That's exactly what I intend to do. I really want to go for it.' The decision was made in an instant.

'In that case,' he said, 'you'd better come and see me.'

After I'd put the phone down, I turned the figures over in my head. Herceptin could raise my chance of survival from 14 per cent to over 50 per cent – more than tripling my hopes of life, in other words. But it could cost £50,000 a year, and it might work more effectively over two years.

Even with my unstoppable optimism, I thought £100,000 would be out of the question. I didn't have that much equity in my house. If I used every penny after settling the mortgage, however, I might be able to raise £25,000 – and six months on Herceptin was better than none. I wasn't too sure where Ash and I would live, but we had good friends – anywhere was better than a box in the ground.

Chapter Nine

I looked around the room. This was my home, and Ash's home. We had lived through dramas here, but we had also shared so many wonderful moments. Many of my happiest memories were associated with this house. This was where my boys had romped and larked about, where Ash had grown in courage and confidence as he learned to trust the world again, where so many troubled youngsters had come for a holiday from their difficult lives.

I didn't want to be parted from this place, but I also knew that I'd leave in an instant if it gave me a good chance of living. It was a tough decision to face, but it wasn't a difficult one to make.

Leaving in an instant, of course, was not an option. My house was in no fit state to be placed on the market. It needed, in estate agents' parlance, 'some attention'. The curtains were in a heap on the sofa, for one thing.

Before my diagnosis, I had decided that redecorating was beyond my ability. The house was always clean and tidy, but to look its best it required work that went beyond my DIY talents. I had booked a firm of decorators and they were halfway through the job – and 'halfway through' is the messiest stage of all.

Ash rolled up his sleeves straight away. He viewed the idea that we might be selling up as an exciting game, and soon he was holding a chair steady as I teetered on it by the window, grappling with curtain rods. By the time Richard dropped round for tea, we had the place looking more presentable. 'There's a reason for all this activity,' I warned him, and explained what Dr Hassan had told me.

Richard was enthusiastic. 'I can't believe no one's told us about this drug before,' he exclaimed.

'This time last week, the trials hadn't been released,' I said. 'In fact, Roche cut the trials short because the early results were so dramatic. I'm among the very first women who could benefit from using Herceptin this way.'

'You'd be crazy to ignore that chance,' he told me emphatically.

'Think about the implications,' I said. 'I know this house belongs to me, but you grew up here. If I sell up to buy a course of Herceptin, I'll be spending all the money I've worked for my entire life, and that ought to be your inheritance.'

Richard said, 'Mum, I just want you alive.'

The decision was made.

A vestige of hope lingered that I might be able to obtain Herceptin on NHS prescription, but that hope was soon dashed. There was no question about it. In the immediate aftermath of the trials, it wasn't even available through private health insurance, though by the time I was able to see the private consultant at his clinic, at the end of May, several insurance companies had already backed down. The results were so emphatic that the insurers could not ignore them . . . but then, the insurance companies did not have to wait for ratification by NICE.

Dr Hassan was an open-minded man whose instinct was to look for solutions, not obstacles, and he suggested I should consider going to India for the drug. I leaped at the idea – I was open to every kind of creative thinking, anything that could reveal a surprise short cut to a solution.

He explained, 'I think the drug could be a lot cheaper in India. It would certainly be cheaper to administer because you'll have to pay for a nurse to come and give it, wherever you are. A private nurse in Britain costs far more than the same service would on the subcontinent. By my calculations you might be better off flying to India once every three weeks. Even taking into account the fares for both you and your son, it might be cheaper than buying it in England. Do some research, have a look at the costs.'

'I'll do it,' I said, 'even if I have to make a hundred flights.'

Still thinking laterally, he asked, 'Have you thought about living over there for a year?'

But there was a limit to how much disruption my family could take. Personally, I would have been prepared to live in the jungles of Borneo for a year if it tripled my chances of living, as Herceptin would do. Ash's health was relatively good at that time, but he would still be too frail to move halfway across the world. In addition, the terms of his residency order would make emigration difficult – though I suspect if I had asked Ash's dad he would have given permission.

My first step was to call the manufacturer, Roche, to

enquire about the cost of the drug in India. I hit an obstacle straight away: Roche couldn't help me by selling the drug to me cheaply. Wherever you went in the world, they explained, the price was set within guidelines. They couldn't have radically different prices for different countries.

Tax regulations did differ from country to country, I discovered from Customs and Excise. If, for example, I sourced the drug in India and imported it to England, I would have to pay VAT on it. That would add 17.5 per cent to the overall cost of having the drug at home, even before I thought of paying a nurse to administer it. If I imported £30,000 of my own Herceptin supplies, I would have to pay duty totalling more than £5,000. I told them that was ridiculous for a life-saving drug.

It was beginning to look as if I really might be better off flying out to India. But that would have been taking a terrible gamble, because I couldn't afford travel insurance – I was quoted £1,000 a week. During chemotherapy, I would be almost uninsurable, because the treatment meant my immune system was not working properly. I was prone to infections and even a stomach bug could have killed me. There was a strong chance the cure would kill me before the cancer could.

Another solution might have been to import it from India to Ireland and take it across to the Isle of Man. I could fly to Douglas every three weeks for my treatment, if that enabled me to get around the VAT and duty. Whether that was legal or not, I didn't even care. I would have done anything, and I couldn't believe any judge would send me to prison for trying to save my own life.

I contacted drug importers to find out if there was any way of bringing it into the country directly to me, rather than through a pharmacy, because the chemists and the private prescriptions all added to the costs. I was disgusted when I found out that the cost to the NHS for a year's course would be £19,500: I would have to pay £27,500 for exactly the same medicine, even before I paid a nurse to administer it. It was less than Dr Hassan's estimate of £50,000, but it was still a staggering amount of money. The NHS were not allowed to sell me the drug at their bulk-buying prices.

I looked into so many possibilities, such as moving to France or Germany: the national health systems in those countries moved much faster than Britain's NHS and Herceptin was already prescribed for early-stage breast cancer. Women in Ireland were getting Herceptin on their medical insurance, but I didn't have that backup.

I could not believe that other European nations were so much more efficient with their healthcare than Britain when our NHS is world-renowned as the first and, supposedly, the best.

Emigrating to the Continent would have been risky, even if I could have persuaded Ash's dad to let me do it. I wasn't sure where I would stand legally – was I entitled to immediate treatment? Because if I wasn't, the delay could kill me. I didn't have time to waste on red tape.

Wherever I turned it was plain I was going to have to do a lot of bargaining.

I was networking, everywhere, day and night, to find out any scrap of information I could. Nobody knew very much about it: 'What drug? What is it? What does it do?'

I was trying to find information frantically because I was literally fighting for my life. I felt that I simply had to have this drug. It was so important to me. I caught myself in the mirror one morning looking particularly ghastly – I was bald, I'd just got out of the shower, and I thought, I look like Gollum out of *Lord of the Rings*. And that's what I was like, desperate for 'my Precious', desperate for this drug.

I wasn't convinced Herceptin would save my life, but I was as certain as I could be that it could extend it. If I could delay the return of the cancer, each year would be a price-less gift. Dr Bryant said, 'In your position, I would fight just as you are doing, but I hope you understand this drug cannot put the clock back. It can't guarantee to make cancer go away for ever. You do realise you are only buying time?'

I told her, 'Yes, that's exactly what I'm doing: I'm buying time. Wouldn't you? Buy time with your children? Even if it only bought me six months I'd pay it. Six hours is precious with my children. What would you have me buy instead?'

I've been told by journalists, by other mums at school, even by people in the street that I must have been mad when I said I would sell my house. They seem to think I was driven out of my mind by panic. But it was the most rational decision I ever took in my life, and I would do the same tomorrow.

At first, I tried to reason with my critics, but I soon saw that they had no conception of the choice I faced. What would they feel like? They had no empathy, no ability to put themselves in that position. They couldn't imagine how it would feel to know their own lives were on the line, to be told they had practically no chance of survival. Most people can't.

I'm not unrealistic; I know I am buying time. Cancer may kill me in the end. Everybody dies sometime, somehow, and perhaps I have been privileged to get a glimpse of what fate has in store for me. I have a chance to prepare my mind and to stave off the inevitable for as long as I can. Each year I can buy is a year of my own life. This drug might buy me five years. It might buy me ten. I might even be one of the rare ones whose cancer never comes back. I'll take my chances and I'll pay no attention to my critics: I am not giving up.

I got in touch with a friend in America, Cessie, who has been a great source of information. She set to work to see if she could purchase Herceptin through the Internet. What she found shocked me – one 'supplier' invited me to pay £611 for a vial of Herceptin in some dosage that Roche didn't even manufacture. If that didn't appeal, I could buy it in tablet form – except there's no such thing, because Herceptin is given intravenously. There were some cynical crooks and conmen out there, preying on the desperate. I was grateful I had enough medical training to spot them.

We are all used to seeing uninvited emails from pharmaceutical merchants, offering our boyfriends and husbands little blue tablets to pep up their appetites. Sexual-performance drugs are not a matter of life and death to most people. Anti-cancer drugs are. I should like to see those suppliers arrested and charged: their actions are tantamount to manslaughter. If I had bought their fake tablets instead of obtaining the real thing, I would probably already be dead.

Cessie also put me on her prayer list, and that meant a lot of Americans were emailing to send me healing wishes. Although I take spiritual issues seriously, I am not an especially religious person; even so, I discovered those messages couldn't fail to lift my hopes every day. It made me feel comforted to know so many people were praying for me.

I was mind-mapping continuously – even though the chemotherapy was making me lose words, and even forget what I was saying in mid-sentence. It was awful: my vision had deteriorated, I couldn't think clearly for any length of time, I couldn't concentrate, but the whole time my mind was sparking all over the place. There was no reasoned approach; I was just looking desperately for a way forward.

There was nothing I wouldn't have tried. I would have gone to the moon if I'd thought it could give me a chance. I made thousands of phone calls . . . I nearly had to sell my house just to pay my phone bill.

By then I knew I needed seventeen doses, which would last me one year, and the bill for the drug alone was going to come to more than £27,000. A further cost was the expense of paying a nurse. I couldn't give Herceptin to myself because it's a dangerous drug and intravenous self-treatment is risky. But by speaking to accountants I discovered I could sidestep VAT if I employed a hospital-at-home service. If I bought the drug privately in the UK and had it at a private hospital, I'd pay VAT; if it was given at my home, I'd save the money. That was a breakthrough. The paradox was this: I would have to pay VAT if I brought the drug into the country myself, even if I was going to administer it at home.

I then tried to get friends who were nurses to agree to administer Herceptin to me, but I couldn't persuade anyone. I understood exactly why they had to say no: they could have lost their registration. I'm always ready to challenge the system, but I can't ask anyone else to take a risk like that.

Throughout these weeks I was on an emotional rollercoaster. Not only did I have the cancer to deal with but I was struggling to give the best possible care to Ash, and to my respite child, too. The frustration and the uncertainties were agony. In my worst nightmares I couldn't have imagined anyone saying to me, 'There is a treatment that could keep you alive, but you can't have it. It doesn't matter how much your family needs you, it's not available to you. If you had money you could have it, but you can't.'

My private consultant, Dr Hassan, gave me unfailing support, but I'm sad to say I did not receive the same backing from my NHS consultant. I wrote to him asking if I could have Herceptin on the NHS, and received a reply saying 'not now, or in the near future.' I prefer not to record his name, but he was a locum consultant – a sort of agency doctor. My impression was that his chief concern was to avoid any disagreements with his employer, the NHS Trust: he didn't want to rock the boat, so he wasn't going to help me at all, at any point.

When I went for my first appointment with him, he made me feel worthless. His whole attitude was summed up with the dismissive words 'The NHS can't afford everything.'

I said, 'But I've got a terminally ill child, I have to stay alive. I'm passionate about staying alive.'

He said, 'So is everyone.'

I was seething when I left his office. I went to my cancer support group and told them, 'He thinks I'm worthless, and I know that I'm worth something. I know I throw myself into life – I have a passion for living that he couldn't possibly imagine.'

I'm not a person who is afraid of death. I am desperate to stay around, but I'm not scared of dying. What I am afraid of is leaving children behind who need me. But that locum consultant made me feel like an insignificant statistic. I can't complain about any of the other doctors, because I have had a lot of support all the way through. But not from him.

It wasn't his fingers on the purse strings. He wasn't the one directly denying me the drug. The point was, it would have helped me hugely if he had come down more heavily on my side. But he didn't.

During my repeated attempts to persuade the NHS to help me obtain Herceptin, I sometimes felt that this doctor and I were locked in personal combat.

I told him, 'I will get this drug.'

He said, 'No, you won't.'

I said, 'You watch me!'

I was going to get it, no matter how – I'd have robbed a bank for it. Because I had to survive. I had to do everything I could to survive.

1 Me with my mother and brother Jim

2 Nana, me (age 10) and brothers Jim and Paul

3 Aged 16

4 Aged 21

5 On honeymoon in the Canaries

6 With mum, my sister and employer Jay in the US.

8 With Richard
aged 18 months

9 Ash and Richard,
May 1997 – first
meeting with Ash

10 With Robert and Ash (aged 6) in Spain

11 On holiday in Tunisia with Richard aged 11

12 Performing North African dance at fête with friend and dance teacher, Jacqui Forster

13 With Richard aged 17, just before diagnosis

14 Person of the month award at Asda – at the start of
the campaign, June 2005

15 Barbara with
Sharon Osbourne –
photo by Ash

16 With the boys, in the garden

Chapter Ten

On 7 June 2005, something extraordinary happened.

One of my friends, Kayleigh Stubbs, had written to our local newspaper, the *Bridgwater Mercury*, nominating me as Reader of the Month. We'd known each other for several years, and she thought I deserved the £50 worth of Asda shopping vouchers – especially because if I won the prize, I could put the money I saved on my weekly shop into my fighting fund. That would be £50 less to find.

The *Mercury* carried her letter on page two: 'Barbara has always been a good friend to me. She likes to help other people and she likes to babysit, as she loves children. Over the years she has fostered many different children with disabilities, and despite being very busy with this demanding work, she is always willing to help her friends. Four months ago, she was diagnosed with cancer. Even under these circumstances, Barbara has remained a cheerful, positive person who always looks on the bright side. Even when she is feeling very ill, she keeps going. No matter how bad things might be, she always puts on a brave face and still manages to find time to spread happiness to other people.'

I was speechless. 'Brave Barbara,' trumpeted the headline. To know we are appreciated by our friends is heart-warming, but to have my praises sung in print brought a lump to my throat. A reporter, Sarah Boobyer, called me to offer the paper's congratulations and to ask me to pose for a photo. I had to warn her that I soon might not be an official *Bridgwater* reader: 'I won't be living here too much longer because I've got to sell my house.'

I didn't give the remark a second thought, until I saw the front page: 'Nurse sells home to buy cancer drugs – breast-cancer victim feels let down by system.'

When I saw the story written down, it somehow seemed more shocking. I saw myself through other people's eyes and I was stirred by the sheer outrage of my own situation. Sarah quoted me: 'As a nurse working on fairly low wages all these years, caring for other people, when you get into trouble yourself there's no help, which I feel is a great shame. I'm not criticising the NHS staff – they've been wonderful. It's the system letting me down.'

I probably said a lot more than that to Sarah, but she'd put her finger on one of the most scandalous aspects. She also summarised the latest financial facts neatly as I understood them at the time: Herceptin would cost me £1,600 a dose, I'd need to take it every three weeks for a year after my chemotherapy ended in October, and the total I was struggling to raise was £27,700.

She also touched on a decision that had slowly dawned on me: this wasn't just my own fight. Thousands of women faced death unless they got Herceptin immediately, and not all of them had houses to sell. Was I going to leave them to it once I'd raised the money for my own treatment, or was I going to keep fighting the system?

'It isn't just about me. I hope to make a difference for

other women because if I keep pushing I can help others in my position.' That's what I told Sarah, and she put it on the front page.

That appeared on the Tuesday morning, 7 June. I bought the *Mercury* first thing and went to my cancer support group, showing it proudly to everybody – 'I'm on the front page!' I thought that was my fifteen minutes of fame.

As I drove home, Sarah rang to say she'd been fielding calls all morning from people who were trying to get hold of me. Could she give out my mobile number and my home telephone number? A wild hope flitted through my mind that some generous billionaire had been moved by my plight and wanted to pay for my treatment. Perhaps Bill Gates or Richard Branson read the *Bridgwater Mercury*.

When I got back to the house, there was no helicopter from Microsoft, but there were two photographers on the doorstep from the *Mail* and the *Express*. I had a wig on, because I'd bought a blonde wig for my blonde days – I had different wigs for different moods – and I was wearing a summer dress.

They asked me to look sad. I said, 'I'm not really a sad person, but I'll do a sad face if you insist.' So I spent five minutes standing outside my house looking miserable, which didn't reflect my state of mind: I was full of fight. The photographers took their pictures . . . and then everything went crazy. I can't describe it any other way.

Before I understood what was happening, the BBC, ITV and Sky News were queuing down the road. All this had erupted because I'd spoken to a reporter on my local paper. This drama had been happening to me for months, and I hadn't been suffering in silence – I'd talked constantly to friends, medical people, Social Services and my cancer support group. I'd told everyone I knew that my house would have to be sold. And then I told one reporter and suddenly the whole world wanted to hear about it.

No one could accuse me of planning my media campaign. My house was in chaos because of the decorating. All my furniture was piled up in the middle of the room. I couldn't let the cameramen film inside, so we had to go into the garden. When I saw the pictures on television, I was mortified: my flowerpots were full of weeds.

Because I'd never done anything on camera before, I blinked continuously. I had a nervous twitch. I stuttered and stammered my way through the interviews, but I managed to complete them without breaking down or running to hide. Maybe it will make a difference, I thought. Maybe people will realise that this drug is available to some people but not to most. It's one law for the rich.

So I stood in front of the cameras and felt sick with fright. No one can imagine how scared I was of going on national news. By the end of the day, I had appeared on all the major news channels, and I thought, Thank God for that. It's over. I've had my day in the limelight. That's my lot. It was unforgettable, but I'm not sure I'd want to go through it again.

In fact, though I had no way of knowing at the time, it was my old life that was over. Until that day, I was an ordinary person, a mother, a neighbour, known by her friends and family and nobody else. After the interviews were broadcast, millions of people knew how desperate my plight was and they all had opinions. The most painful part of my life had become public property.

When the next morning's papers appeared in the newsagent's, my story was in the *Mail*, London's *Metro*, *Express* and the *Western Daily Press*. Local radio stations were phoning me, and the postman practically needed a wheelbarrow to deliver my letters because the *Mercury* had printed my address. The following day, more of the nationals ran it, I was on the TV news again, Radio 2 rang up to ask if I'd do *The Jeremy Vine Show*, and my head was spinning.

This was clearly too good an opportunity to waste. I contacted Roche and said, 'I'm going on the radio, on Jeremy Vine's show in the morning on Radio 2. It's just about the biggest radio programme in Britain, with millions upon millions of listeners, and I do not want to make a fool of myself by getting my facts wrong. I need to know this drug inside out. I need to understand the results of the trials. Can you help me?'

I had heard rumours that Roche would offer the drug for nothing to people who generated publicity for them, but I was soon to discover that the rumours were unfounded. Roche was willing to give me explanations and information when I asked for it, but never offered any help to get the drug.

The morning of *The Jeremy Vine Show*, my heart was in my mouth. I needn't have worried – everyone was marvellous, and not just at the BBC building itself. The audience, all the people who listened, rallied round. From that show alone, over the course of the next two months, £7,000 would come in.

My friends Gina and Kayleigh quickly helped me to open a charity account, the Herceptin Treatment Fund, though I wasn't able to set up a registered charity: that would have taken about a year. We knew I would need the money soon. It was already early June and by September I would have to have raised the financing, ready for the end of my chemotheraphy in October.

Even at that point, conventional fundraising looked impossible. I was not going to collect £27,700 in three months with sponsored walks and bike rides. I couldn't even stand on a street corner and shake a tin. Selling the house still seemed my only option.

But money started coming in. I was invited on *This Morning*, *GMTV* and a series of other television programmes. I was on the radio continuously. It passed in a blur: chemotherapy was playing havoc with my brain and my energy levels.

By then I'd had twelve doses – four toxic ones that had turned my skin orange, and eight that were less virulent but still unpleasantly poisonous. They targeted fast-growing cells indiscriminately, from cancer cells to brain cells, and side effects such as mouth ulcers were the least of my problems.

I'd stagger down the stairs to pick up the phone, make a note of the next radio interview I was booked to do, then scramble back to the bathroom to take another close look at the porcelain.

The emails and letters were flooding in, many with cheques or pledges of cash. One Radio 2 listener sent £500, an act of generosity that just floored me. The woman who sent it told me her mother had suffered from breast cancer before her death earlier that year, aged ninety-four: 'I would like you to have part of the money she left me, in her memory.' I was too choked to speak.

Many other people were just as generous, even if they could not afford to send nearly as much. Every pound was deeply appreciated by me.

Sometimes the letters that came with just £1 were more moving than those that came with £50. One or two even sent £1,000. Many of them were written by people with cancer themselves, elderly people in their eighties, on tight pensions, who sent me a precious pound.

I wish I could print all their letters. Many left me in tears. I wasn't crying because the fight was so exhausting, or because I might die despite the generosity of all these strangers; I was crying because I had never suspected there were so many kind and loving people in the world who were willing to help a woman they had never even met.

One lady in Leeds sent me £25 which she had raised by making greetings cards. 'I have lost family and friends to cancer,' she wrote, 'and have been actively raising money for cancer charities for many years now.'

A man in Merseyside enclosed a cheque for £100, adding, 'I wish you and your family all the luck in the world. Please do not feel the need to reply, as this will eat into your funds.' He plainly knew the value of a stamp, and yet had the bigness of heart to send so much money. What a gift: it literally was the gift of life.

The local golf club, Enmore Park, which had raised funds for the breast-care unit at Musgrove Park Hospital in

Taunton the previous year, sent £1,000. Uri Geller sent the same amount.

'I was moved and, at the same time, disgusted by your plight,' wrote one lady who sent £25 ('Receipt not required – save the postage!'). Another who sent £10 told me, 'My daughter had a rare liver cancer when she was eleven years old. She is now thirty-three and has a baby of her own. I don't have much to give away, but I hope your appeal amounts to loads of money.'

I had letters that were addressed to 'Barbara Clark, Bridgwater' and even those reached me. One of the newspapers printed the wrong address but the letters were still arriving: Royal Mail realised that I wasn't at the other address, so they just redirected them.

The postman deserves a special mention. He must have been fed up of me – I expect he got weak knees from dragging around all my sacks of post.

One irate correspondent sent £100 and said, 'This is entirely wrong of me – you are an Englishwoman and the NHS should be using its funds to sort out your medical problem. Instead, it is spending its money and time (paid for by British taxpayers) on medical tourists. Because I – and I am sure many others – am supporting you, there will be even more funds available for these tourists.'

Yet at the end of letter, he added, 'I shall keep an eye on your website. If you do not reach the required sum by January, please tell me.'

That was proof to me, if more proof were needed, that people were giving from their hearts and not their heads. Their response was completely emotional.

One woman told me her daughter was getting Herceptin, which meant she was in the later stages of breast cancer. She had had a mastectomy the previous year, but the cancer had returned twelve months later. She had two children, aged fourteen and ten.

Another wrote, 'I shall be eighty-one in a few weeks time and I had a mastectomy of my right breast twenty-five years ago, so I have been very lucky to be able to see my three children grow up and marry and have grandchildren. Now I have four great-grandchildren.'

Perhaps the letter that summed them all up came from a woman who apologised for being unable to send a large donation and then sent several pounds, which I am certain was more than she could afford. 'Life is priceless,' she wrote.

The letters and emails came flooding in faster than I could reply. One day during that first week, I got 301 emails. That was a record, but it wasn't unusual to have more than 200. So many people sent me money, encouragement and prayers that I couldn't write back to them all.

The letters and emails were also arriving faster than I could organise them. What I needed was a pair of filing cabinets, with a filing clerk to go with them; what I had was a mountain of mail on my dining table. The pressure of the constant media attention, the mental havoc wreaked by chemotherapy and the day-to-day demands of my family were overwhelming me. When I realised I might have replied to some letters twice, or not at all, I felt distraught. If I'd had any hair, I would have been tearing it out.

A couple of children sent their pocket money – how

could I fail to reply to that? And yet somebody else would send £500 and I might have missed that letter by replying to the little ones that touched my heart. If any reader sent me a donation, or a letter of prayers and best wishes, and did not receive a reply, please accept my sincere apologies. I truly appreciated every word of support, and every penny.

After a dose of chemotherapy I could be prostrate for a week, yet even then I would force myself to get up and try to write replies. If the phone stopped ringing for a couple of hours, which it rarely did, I might manage five or ten replies, but that barely dented the dozens that arrived each morning. If I were able to work a computer, that might have helped, but this was not the time to be attending evening classes in information technology – I can pick up emails but that's the limit of my ability with a PC.

Unable even to make my computer's printer function reliably, I was having to write every reply by hand. The chemotherapy drip was going into my right hand, which had become stiff and painful – in fact, it hurt right up the arm. Gripping my pen and gritting my teeth, I did reply to hundreds . . . but I'm sure there were far too many that I missed.

My friend Andrew, the hynotherapist, came round one day and saw this mountain of unanswered letters. He was alarmed. I told him, 'I can't cope. I'm floundering. I'm trying to write back and thank people, but I'll never answer them all. It's out of control. Please help me to pick out the ones who need replies.'

I'm afraid some of them got a standard reply, sent by

Andrew, who gathered up about a hundred letters and sent a pro forma answer. What else could we do? I'm hopeless with paperwork at the best of times and this wasn't the best of times.

It was an impossible situation. There was more going on in my life than three people could have coped with. I was filming all the time, doing radio and newspaper interviews, trying to cope with chemotherapy and throwing up every ten minutes, and I was faced with this surge of letters and emails every day.

In short, I was running around like a headless chicken. I simply couldn't get on top of it. I needed a secretary, an agent and a personal assistant. Sometimes, while they were filming me, the journalists were answering my phones: 'You're from the BBC, are you? She can't talk to you right now, she's filming for us. Who are we? Sky News!'

The cameramen grinned at me and said my life had gone crazy, and it had.

There were several days when I counted more than sixty phone calls. I'd never experienced anything like it, and it was just exhausting. Perhaps if you're a stock dealer or a Hollywood fixer, you thrive on the adrenaline of constant phone calls. I didn't. I wanted to scream.

In February 2006, I managed to take Ash away for a few days, but I knew the rest of my life couldn't be put on hold. Even though this was long after the initial rush of publicity, the media attention was still head-splitting. I asked a neighbour to drop round to my house while we were away, because I knew my answer machine would be filled on the first day. She cleared forty-five calls from my voicemail that day, noting down all the messages. When I came back, she was looking at me with different eyes. 'Now I know what you do with your life,' she said.

Not all missed calls are the same – I discovered they have their own hierarchy. Some people will call you straight back because they need an urgent answer. Some people will forget you as soon as their deadline passes: you call them and they have lost all interest in whatever they once needed to say. Others will follow through with efficient emails, and a few will simply bombard your phone with repeated calls because they can't take 'no' for an answer.

As well as the journalists, many ordinary people were ringing because they wanted to give me encouragement. After an interview on Radio 4, seventeen people called me. Most of them were cancer sufferers themselves who wanted to know if Herceptin could help them too. I didn't mind offering advice – my nurse's instincts kicked in – but I was worried about the man who rang to say he wanted to spend a day in London Zoo's bear enclosure to help me raise money. That sounded a bad idea to me – I didn't want my supporters to be eaten alive.

I wasn't having to cope alone, of course. One person I can't thank enough is Sarah Boobyer of the *Mercury*. She was the mover and shaker, and I couldn't have done it without her.

Not only was she the one who broke my story, she's put me in the *Mercury* nearly every week since, as she campaigned tirelessly to try and save my life. She came up with the slogan 'Send a Pound to Save Barbara'. And I was overwhelmed with half a sackload of letters every day, all of them containing between £1 and £5, small donations from people who cared. It was very moving.

By the middle of July 2005 the money in the fighting fund was swelling so fast that a new hope began to grow in my mind. 'For the first time,' I told Sarah, 'I think I might be able to fund a course of Herceptin without selling my house.'

Chapter Eleven

I believe we're all on earth for a reason. As a nurse and foster carer, I felt I was living my life for a purpose, and that purpose was to look after Ash. In the human jigsaw of six billion pieces, that's where I fitted in. As long as Ash needed me, I would be there to care for him and give him all the support he required. That's why I found the cancer diagnosis so hard to deal with. It turned everything I believed on its head. To discover I had such a virulent cancer, with so little chance of survival, was more than cruel. It robbed my life of its point. It mocked the most important truth in my world: the knowledge that Ash needed me.

I thought about this intently, and discussed it with my friends. Gradually, as I realised how many people were touched by my story, I began to understand that this ordeal wasn't pointless. On the contrary, it gave me a new purpose, another reason to stay alive.

Many people will find this hard to believe, or even to understand, but part of me is now glad that I got the disease – glad, at least, that I had the chance to tackle the most daunting, desperate fight of my life. If I hadn't had cancer, and not been insured privately, I couldn't have raised national awareness of the scandalous state of cancer care within the NHS. I couldn't have given so many other women hope.

When I started my fight, there was a black hole where hope should have been. As Sarah put it pithily, 'Bizarrely, Barbara will not be given the drug until her case becomes terminal – a cruel paradox.'

An army of people quickly rallied, eager to fight alongside me. One of the most prominent was Ian Liddell-Grainger, the MP for Bridgwater. Three weeks after my story broke, he raised my case in the House of Commons. Though I was so ill I could barely face the bus journey down the M4, I forced myself to attend. It was one of the most exciting and stressful days of my life. I was sitting in the Commons gallery, listening to the most powerful people in the country debate an issue that I had raised and citing my name to emphasise their arguments. I had achieved a great deal by provoking the debate, but it was strange to hear my personal ordeal discussed and be unable to contribute.

Ian's demand was simple: he wanted the government to order NICE to fast-track approval for Herceptin. Fast-tracking, of course, isn't what NICE does. The longer they delay approval for a new drug, the more money the NHS can save . . . and the fewer lives. That summary might sound cynical and simplistic, but it is undeniable that the will is lacking within NICE to address delays. Although Herceptin was being prescribed in Europe and America, NICE had not yet acted, and the slower their wheels turned, the longer this expensive miracle drug was being kept off the NHS books.

I wish I had Ian's eloquence. I know I can get my point across, especially when I feel strongly about an issue, but Ian can take an argument to pieces and lay it out on the table like nuts and bolts. It's a remarkable gift. He made his case in the Commons with elegant force.

The US, Canada, France and Germany had all bypassed their own drug licensing laws to make Herceptin available to breast-cancer patients as soon as the Roche trials revealed it could halt the disease's spread during its early stages. There were more than 40,000 women with breast cancer diagnosed each year in the UK, Ian explained, and it was a disease that could affect men as well as women.

'Britain has a valued reputation for scrupulous examination of any new drug,' he said. 'But this is a matter of life and death. The people who might benefit from Herceptin are not at all scared by any small risks which might be associated with taking it. If I had a fast-moving HER2 cancer, I would be doing precisely what Barbara Clark is doing.'

If the government did nothing, he warned, I would die – and so would 'hundreds of brave Barbara Clarks'.

The parliamentary undersecretary for the Department of Health, Liam Byrne, stood up to defend the government: 'Over the next ten years, we will make extraordinary progress in the war on cancer,' he promised.

I wanted to stand up and warn the minister that I wasn't going to live another ten years, or even another two, if he and his colleagues didn't pull their fingers out.

'I do not want Mrs Clark to have to sell her home to get Herceptin,' he said, 'but equally we cannot override the licensing process so that a drug is licensed before trial data has been properly reviewed and side effects fully understood.

'I believe that as new drugs are developed, we will turn

again and again to the ethical dilemma at the heart of this debate. How do we balance the possibility of introducing the benefits that new drugs bring as fast as humanely possible with the need to ensure that the new drugs are safe and without downsides that undermine the very reasons for their prescription?'

I understood his point: doctors could only hand out drugs if they were certain that the medicine would do much more good than harm. But Herceptin was already used for cancer's terminal stages. The drug had effectively been tested on human guinea pigs with little to lose, and though there was a known risk of heart problems, there were no real blind spots. Doctors knew what this drug did; it was not an unknown quantity. Moreover, chemotherapy causes many more problems than Herceptin.

Ian put pressure on civil servants and fellow MPs to give him the full picture about the licensing process, and we discovered that arrangements were already being made within the NHS to review the drug as soon as it won a European licence and got official clearance in this country. The licence would be granted possibly by 2006, but NICE's approval process could take five further years. If I didn't get this growth receptor inhibitor by October 2005, the odds were six to one that my cancer would be back by the middle of 2006 – and this time it would be incurable.

I called Sarah after the debate and told her, 'I'm feeling very positive. Every month that we bring the process forward, we save another two hundred and fifty lives. I don't know those women – most of them probably don't even have cancer yet. They might not even have been diagnosed.

But they exist, they have families and loved ones, they might have children, they might be pregnant – whoever they are, we have to help them live.'

Sarah asked if I had enjoyed the day.

'It was very productive,' I said, 'but also very tiring. Ian was fantastic and I am so grateful.'

Sarah reprinted the paper's appeal, urging every reader to donate a pound. Publicity was clearly the answer to my fundraising problems. A few days after the Commons debate, my fund stood at £4,823. But there was a huge distance still to go – more than £22,000 – and unless I could keep the news in the forefront of people's minds, my fight would start to falter. Without publicity, the NHS bean-counters could quietly put Herceptin back on hold and save money while people died.

I had already managed to get myself on national BBC radio – Radio 1, 2, 4 and 5 . . . If I played the piano, I could probably have been on Radio 3 as well.

I'd been on the local stations, the independents, Spanish radio, French radio, Canadian radio, and I'd appeared on TV screens on just about all the news channels, from Sky to BBC News 24. Over the next few weeks friends rang to say they'd seen me on Sky television in Malta, the Canaries, France and Canada.

In my determination to get the treatment to save my life, I tried every avenue. I was unstoppable in my desperation to stay alive, in my passion. I sometimes think this book should be called *A Passion for Life*, because nobody wanted it more than me. I know everybody wants life, but I was going to do anything to get this drug.

I racked my brains to come up with new angles that would keep my fight on the front pages, and an outrageous idea began to take shape in my mind. I was going to start my course by October, no matter what – I had the money to start the course, if not yet for the full treatment. But why should I have the drug behind closed doors?

Herceptin is a dangerous drug to administer, especially when it's given for the first time. There's a one in 200 risk of cardiac failure, which can of course be fatal though it hasn't happened to date. But if I couldn't get Herceptin on the NHS, and I couldn't afford a private nurse to wield the needle, and none of my friends dared put their licences on the line . . . then I was going to have to administer it to myself.

I had an accomplice in my friend Gina. She was prepared to stand beside me and do whatever she could to help in an untrained capacity. But she couldn't hold the needle, and that highlighted my biggest worry: how was I going to self-administer the drug?

Herceptin is given intravenously, which meant the drip would have to flow into a vein in my right hand. I am entirely right-handed. Because I have had lymph nodes removed from under my left arm, it's not possible for me to have an intravenous injection in my left arm. The whole arm could swell up badly. The problem is so serious that I will never even be able to have my blood pressure taken on that side.

It would have been hard for me to guide the needle left-handed – think how difficult it is to simply write your name with your 'wrong hand'. Now think about how you'd feel with your whole life at stake as your wrong hand guided a needle into your vein.

I decided I could do it. I knew I would need someone to put the banding on and hold my arm. I would have to find a vein. I've done the course on venipuncture, but I've never administered drugs intravenously, so I read up on it.

With Gina there, I was confident I could take the risk.

I was going to be scared out of my wits when I gave myself the first dose, but at the same time I knew it was my best chance of life. Why hide a drama like that?

At first, I thought of inviting a news crew into my living room. I could imagine the reporters whispering into their microphones like snooker commentators as the drug dripped into my bloodstream. Then I imagined the chaos if I had a heart attack. I didn't want to die on Sky News.

That's when I had a brainwave: I'll sit in the car park of Taunton Hospital, outside Accident and Emergency, and do it there. That should be safer.

The idea had three benefits. Firstly, it was highly symbolic. I was being refused the treatment I needed through the state system, even though I'd worked for it since my twenties. Secondly, and more practically, I would be close to the resuscitation teams if I did suffer cardiac failure. Thirdly, the hospital administrators might be so embarrassed by the furore that they would provide a trained nurse to give me the drug inside the building. The latter was my secret hope, but I realised it was in vain: I had already established that I couldn't have the drug on hospital premises, even if I did administer it to myself. Apart from the VAT issue, there were NHS rules about private drugs being adminstered in state hospitals.

So the car park it would be. That's how determined I was

to highlight the injustices of the system. I was going to make the most possible fuss. This would be Russian roulette in front of the cameras.

I told reporters my plan, and one wanted to know 'What happens if you collapse?'

I didn't have an answer to that – at least, not one that could subdue the fear in the pit of my stomach. I just prayed that I would be close enough to A&E to stand a chance of survival.

The reporters were sceptical about the whole project. 'The car park?' they said. 'The hospital will never allow it.'

I was determined to force the issue, so I spoke to Dr Bryant. After consulting with her managers, she called me back. 'We're going to have to let you do it because legally we cannot give you that drug in this building.'

My stomach lurched. I thought, Oh, no, they're going to let me do this. I'm going to have to go through with it!

In the end, that degree of drama wasn't necessary. It would have made fantastic TV, though. There's nothing like having a suspected heart attack on national telly to generate headlines – and, ultimately, save lives.

Meanwhile, there was urgent fundraising going on. By the end of July I had raised almost £8,000 and was getting into my stride.

It wasn't just my family and friends who were fighting by my side. My neighbours have been marvellous, too. Pauline, who lived across the road, has been there for me from the beginning. She came and visited me in hospital when I said I didn't want visitors because I was depressed. There was no nonsense with her. Gina came too and the pair of them told me, 'You're perfectly all right. You're exactly the same person you were before the op, and we care about you.'

Pauline and I weren't particularly close before all of this started, but over the months her dedication has been touching and inspiring. She's attended everything that I've organised, and she's always calling in to check that I am all right. Their practical help has been invaluable, too: for instance, Pauline and her husband built a ramp at the front of the house for my respite child's wheelchair.

Best of all, though, has been the endless love and support I've had from Richard and Ash. Richard astonished me one afternoon when he announced, 'Mum, I'm going to do a sky-dive for you.'

I said, 'Don't be silly, Richard, you've only got to go three steps up a ladder and you feel dizzy.' He is absolutely terrified of heights.

He meant it, though. 'I want to do the thing that I'm most scared of, to show you how much I love you.'

Richard works at Brandon's Tool Hire in Bridgwater. Originally, several of his colleagues wanted to do it, too, but one by one they pulled out. That left just Richard, and his nerves were getting worse by the day.

His boss, Julian, told me, 'Barbara, I cannot watch that boy do it alone. I'm going to do the jump with him.'

Right up to the day of the jump itself, I didn't fully believe Richard was going to go through with it. We arrived at Dunkeswell Airfield, near Honiton in Devon, and Julian went up in the light aircraft first. Poor Richard faced a long wait for his turn.

He kept walking off. He was so nervous I was worried he might let everybody down at the last minute, and his girlfriend, Laura, who is a very pretty girl, had tears in her eyes. I understood, because I couldn't have done the jump myself. We kept urging him on: 'Come on, Richard, you can do this.'

'I can't, I can't,' he said. He kept wandering off so far I thought he was going to need a cab to get back.

Eventually, he got in the light aircraft, but before they took off, Ash, like a typical little brother, went up to the instructor and said, 'Spin him on the way down!'

We saw him jump and he was spinning all the way down. I thought, He's never going to speak to Ash again. He's going to hate him for ever.

He reached the ground, we ran over, and he said, 'Wow! That was fantastic!' We all nearly fainted. He'd been terrified for so long, saying, 'I don't want to go up,' but for days afterwards he was looking up at the sky and murmuring, 'Wow! I've been up there.'

It was a terrific day, with lovely weather. I took dozens of photos. Kayleigh worked hard, encouraging people to be sponsors, and altogether the jump raised around £1,500.

At the same time, one of my neighbour's sons, a quiet fourteen-year-old named David Faulkner, decided to do a sponsored swim. He swam for an hour and a half. I went to watch him, and his mum was there, counting the lengths; by the time he finished I was almost in tears. It made me very emotional that people would do all this to help me. David raised almost £400 by swimming 3,000 metres, which is about two miles, or 120 lengths. The pictures of that event are still up in the school. His mum was so proud of him, and so was I.

The afternoon before Richard and Julian's parachute jump, we held a fund-raising barbecue at Gina's small-holding. Sixty people turned up and paid £5 a head, though the weather was pretty miserable. My brother Paul came from Essex to cook – he brought the barbecue equipment – and my sister came all the way from Hampshire to do face-painting.

We had pony rides and a bouncy castle, most of which was arranged by Gina. The award-winning local butcher Pynes provided all the meat at cost price, and we tucked into delicious burgers and sausages. I used my Asda vouchers to get the bread rolls. Brandon's Tool Hire provided the toilets, Gerber Foods donated all the drinks, and my neighbour Marion, who runs a wine merchant's, supplied the wine and beer at cost. We did very well on that deal!

At the beginning of September, we held an auction of promises, where bidders could compete for lots such as an evening in a limo, a paintballing session for ten, a 1956 cricket bat signed by the Australian team and lunch for two with Ian Liddell-Grainger at the House of Commons.

Sarah Boobyer rang round all the businesses in Bridgwater to drum up donations, and she helped me print up flyers to advertise the event. There was my face, above the *Mercury*'s 'Fighting for Barbara' slogan, and the date, place and time of the auction.

It looked great – but flyers don't hand themselves out. I had to go into town on the morning of the auction and hand the leaflets out myself, together with Ash and some of the children from our road.

Unfortunately, people don't know what you're out there for, so they walk past you. There you are with your leaflets, desperate to find people who can help, but the shoppers walking by don't know you're trying to save your life. They just stream past: 'No, thank you. No, thank you.' Or they take a leaflet and drop it straight in the bin. Ash kept on retrieving them from the bin and flattening them out.

I have never been so humiliated in my life. I was mortified. I was nearly in tears with embarrassment, especially because I was doing it on my own, the only adult with a group of children. I might as well have sat on the streets like a beggar, because that was what I felt like. In fact, that was another idea I had – I was going to sit on the streets of London and beg for my life, like a heroin addict. I had teamed up with Dorothy Griffiths, another Herceptin campaigner, and we decided we could really do it: sit on the pavement and beg for our drug treatment. And hopefully get arrested, just to try and raise awareness.

Of course I would have had to make arrangements for someone to look after Ash while I was in a police cell. It probably wasn't such a clever plan, but it illustrates how there were no limits to our fundraising ideas.

Dorothy Griffiths lives in Stoke-on-Trent and was one of the first people in the country to get Herceptin for late-stage breast cancer, in 2001. Although she was given just six months to live, she's still going strong, enjoying life and fighting to help others. Part of that is because of Herceptin. She's taken up the battle for everyone with early-stage breast cancer, and she started a charity, the Dorothy Griffiths Breast Cancer Appeal Fund, to help women in her area through their treatment.

She's dynamic and great fun, and she always makes me feel good after I've spoken with her. We first met after I appeared on ITV's *This Morning*: she emailed the producers to explain she had been campaigning for Herceptin for a long time, and her email was forwarded to me. We were able to get together when she was on her way home from a summer holiday in Cornwall – we met in a service station on the M5. One of my local papers, the *Bridgwater Times*, took a photo of us sitting on a grass embankment planning our campaigns.

In the end, the auction was a great success. It raised in the region of £2,500. My neighbour Marion bought the lunch with Ian Liddell-Grainger, who joined us for the bidding. Marion said he really made a day of it with a four-hour tour of the Commons and the Lords, and then out for a slap-up lunch. That's just one example of how much Ian, and so many others, have helped.

Chapter Twelve

The fight of my life had become a national campaign with a significance that went far beyond my own struggle. What had begun as an emotional drama was now a political scenario, played out on primetime news and on the front pages of Fleet Street newspapers.

In order to maintain the momentum, I had to achieve political victories. My first had come when Ian Liddell-Grainger had forced the Commons debate on Herceptin that had dragged the issue out into the open. No one in government could feign ignorance any longer.

The next major win happened much sooner than expected, at the end of July 2005. Health Secretary Patricia Hewitt came forward to state publicly what we had suspected a few weeks earlier: the licensing authorities were coming under pressure from Whitehall to give the go-ahead for Herceptin as soon as possible.

But Ms Hewitt went one step further by announcing the drug would be fast-tracked. That meant the red tape would be swept aside and NICE would be told to start assessing the drug as soon as it was licensed in Europe. NICE's assessment was expected to take anything from a year to five years, so it would be little use to me directly, but knowing that thousands of lives would be saved gave me a huge boost. Whatever happened to me personally, my furious campaigning had achieved action. The impact of my appeals on radio and television could be measured in human lives.

The health secretary told reporters, 'I have the deepest sympathy for the pain and suffering that cancer patients and their families experience, and completely understand why they want to see any drug that can help being made more widely available.'

The boldness of that statement won her a lot of friends and admirers, including me, and was welcomed by cancer charities and doctors alike. I appreciate that Ms Hewitt is a politician and that she has to say what's expedient, but I honestly believe she was sincere about this. She wanted to do the right thing.

I felt as if I was pushing a boulder up a mountain and I'd just felt it roll forward. By the middle of August my fighting fund had topped £15,000. But while I had been busy fundraising, I had received a series of intriguing emails.

The first email had come some time before, when I had been interviewed on *The Jeremy Vine Show*. It was from a woman named Michelle Wood and her partner, Paul. They assessed my situation point by point and concluded, 'We believe you have a strong case under the Human Rights Act.'

I had glanced at their credentials, seen that they weren't lawyers, though they had studied law. It had been one of about 300 emails I had received that day, and I'm afraid I simply deleted it.

I can't blame myself for that. Even the government's

lawyers were slow to wake up to the legal implications of my case. How Michelle and her partner spotted it so quickly I shall never understand – they must be highly astute. The truth is, I took no notice of it at all. I was getting plenty of emails urging me to embrace religious solutions or submit to diet and health regimes. So many people were contacting me to tell me about alternative cures for cancer that I sometimes felt as though I'd read about every cure that was ever suggested, and it quickly got to the stage where I skimmed emails without reading them closely.

Michelle was persistent, however. She continued to drop me a line or two, reminding me that the Human Rights Act was there to be used. And I kept emailing back to thank her for her interest, but I still didn't pay serious attention.

At the beginning of August, the papers were full of the story of Sheikh Omar Bakri Mohammed, the radical Muslim cleric who had fled London in the wake of the 7/7 bombings. He needed a heart operation, and there was talk that if he decided to return to Britain, the NHS could not refuse to treat him, even though he was not a British national.

Michelle emailed me again: 'You do realise why the NHS can't turn him away, don't you? It's a human-rights issue. He has a fundamental right to life. And so do you.'

And that's when it really dawned on me.

That's it, I realised. I've got a case under the Human Rights Act. My right to life is laid down in law. Michelle has actually got a point. Even though she's not a solicitor, she certainly knows her stuff.

So I rang a reporter I knew called Martyn Halle and told

him, 'I'm going to take the country to court under the Human Rights Act.'

He really wasn't interested. He'd reached the stage with my story where he was bored to tears with it. I thought he was a *Sunday Telegraph* reporter, though I later realised he was a freelance. I tried to persuade him to run the story, but he said, 'Yeah, well, Barbara, you've had a lot of publicity. I'll have a think about it.' And that was it for my latest brainwave.

I wasn't discouraged. I was having brainwaves all the time, I was so desperate. If one wild idea didn't help me get Herceptin, the next one might.

He rang me back a couple of days later and, though he still didn't sound too excited, said, 'I've had a think about it and I think maybe I will cover the story. The problem is, I can't write about you because you've had too much publicity. Can you think of anybody else who could feature in the story?'

I said, 'Get in touch with Dorothy Griffiths. She's a seasoned campaigner and she'll certainly be able to put you in touch with someone.' I was grateful for the effort I'd put into establishing contacts with people as diverse as Martyn and Dorothy, because they were now paying dividends.

Martyn said he was intending to write something for the *Sunday Telegraph* that weekend, on 21 August 2005. When the story was printed, it felt like another small step in the right direction, though not an especially significant one. Martin had talked to a solicitor, Stephen Grosz, who agreed there might be a case to be answered in court.

'A group of women suffering from breast cancer are

planning to invoke the Human Rights Act in order to receive the latest treatment,' Martyn wrote. 'They are prepared to go to the High Court [. . .] The act states that everyone is entitled to the right of life, and the women are claiming that their right to life is being infringed by not being able to have Herceptin.'

There were some strong quotes from Dorothy: 'What patients find difficult to accept is that this drug is now available privately in the UK through BUPA [the private health company] but is not available on the NHS. If doctors working for BUPA think it is safe – which they must – why is the NHS holding back? This is clearly to do with money and not safety issues.'

But it was what Stephen Grosz, a partner in the London law firm Bindman & Partners, said that really made me sit up: 'If you can prove that a drug treatment is effective and that your life is being curtailed by you not being allowed to have that drug that could save your life, then you would probably succeed.'

Martyn had also unearthed a heartbreaking story about a thirty-five-year-old woman in Bishop's Stortford, Hertfordshire, who had been diagnosed with inflammatory breast cancer eight weeks earlier. She had a two-year-old son and was expecting her second child in a few weeks, but doctors had given her no better than a 30 per cent chance of survival.

With Herceptin, her odds were better than fifty-fifty. Her hospital, Addenbrooke's, in Cambridge, had issued a statement: 'We are aware from recent trials in America that Herceptin is an effective new treatment for early breast cancer. However, Herceptin has not been licensed for this new indication, nor has it been appraised by NICE. Until it has been, we cannot offer this treatment to our patients.'

I thought it was a great bit of reporting that couldn't fail to keep NICE focused on the fast track. Later that day, however, Martyn rang me at home to say, 'I'm absolutely furious. They pulled it from the later editions of the paper. It was a good story, but the Department of Health leaned on them and the news desk pulled it from the London editions.'

Well, that did it. All the alarm bells were ringing, the lights were flashing. I could no longer miss what Michelle had been trying so patiently to make me understand: I had a case. In fact, my case was so strong I had the Department of Health on alert.

I called Stephen Grosz at Bindman & Partners and told him I was the woman who had tipped off the reporter about this human-rights angle. 'Do you think I have got a case?' I asked.

'Well,' he said, 'it's never been done before. I don't see why you wouldn't have a case. Would you like to come and talk to me?'

So I went straight to London. Stephen Grosz impressed me immediately with his gentle manner, ready smile and rapid grasp of the facts. 'Do you know,' he said, 'I think you're right! You have a fundamental right to human life and this drug could be your only realistic hope.'

I could have hugged him, if I hadn't felt so weak.

We went through the main points of my argument: 'If Herceptin can be proved to be available in other countries, as it is – it's used throughout North America, including Canada, and in Europe – and I can prove that this would dramatically improve my odds . . . and remember my odds are probably the worst of anybody with an HER2 tumour,' I said, 'then I think I've got a case under the Human Rights Act.'

Stephen was thinking tactically. 'Before we try that route,' he said, 'let's write to the health authority, to the NHS Trust itself. After all, you have a child with a life-limiting illness and I think you might get the drug on the criterion of exceptional need.'

Most of my contact with the NHS had been conducted through my consultant oncologist, Dr Hassan, with letters flying backwards and forwards, and this was practically the first time anybody had suggested taking the fight to the primary care NHS trust which governed all my local health services.

'Bear in mind,' said Stephen, 'that it could be difficult to get legal aid: because of the money you have raised, you might not qualify for financial assistance with your case. But you can't afford to bring this fight to court on your own – you need to hang on to every penny you've got because you might need it to pay for Herceptin.'

It was a dilemma. 'What do you suggest?' I asked.

'Before we move straight to court, let's try approaching Somerset Coast Primary Care Trust [PCT]. We'll give them due warning – if they don't back down and prescribe this drug for you, we're taking them to court. Let's make sure they know that.'

The trust's response to Stephen's letter was quite

shocking: they seemed never to have heard of me. The locum consultant I had met earlier in the year had not even bothered to contact them about my request for Herceptin. It appeared he had decided that since the drug was unlicensed and unapproved, he didn't have to provide it, so he had sent me a letter saying I couldn't have it, now or in the near future, without even trying to help me.

I said to Stephen Grosz, 'They can't refuse it to me on these grounds, that it's unlicensed and unapproved by NICE, because they are already providing drugs for my son that are equally unlicensed and unapproved. There's lots of medication that falls into that category. I should know: I'm a nurse. So it's nonsense. They can prescribe Herceptin if they want to.'

To back up my argument, I had a statement from Patricia Hewitt in which she bluntly stated that drugs did not have to be licensed or approved before they could be prescribed. I was starting to really like this health secretary. The cancer tsar Mike Richards had also said that unlicensed drugs could be prescribed in exceptional circumstances.

I surveyed my arsenal. As well as Patricia Hewitt's statement, I had the backing of the media and the experience I had gained from caring for Ash, and I had the best human-rights lawyer in London.

By the middle of September the press were scenting a landmark victory. The *Observer* called me and I told them that I would be able to get Herceptin on prescription but not until the cancer came back, by which time I would be incurable. 'I always thought my role in life was to look after my son to the end,' I said angrily. 'I'm spurred on by sheer desperation. The NHS know there is a treatment that could save my life, but they refuse to pay for it; I am horrified they could be so heartless. The consultant said that the NHS can't pay for everything; but can't they prioritise life-saving treatment?'

'I am not going to stand back and let hundreds of women die,' I told the reporter. 'I am legally challenging the NHS because it is limiting my right to life. Under the Human Rights Act, everyone has a right to life. If there is a life-saving drug out there, then I and thousands of other women should be able to have it.' The *Observer* then printed a long article that gave me more space to explain my aims than I usually got on television.

The *Daily Mail* picked up the story the following day, and my phone was once again ringing off the hook. Stephen Grosz felt publicity like this could not fail to tighten the pressure on the trust.

We then wrote to the PCT, which replied by saying they would hear my case at the Exceptional Needs Committee at the end of September.

That certainly would not have happened if Stephen had not threatened the PCT with the High Court. Suddenly, I was on their list of priorities. It boded well, but I was baffled that a committee of executives and managers thought they had the right to judge whose need was exceptional, whose life mattered more than most.

While all of this had been going on, my fund had been rising. It now stood at £25,000 – very nearly enough to cover my course. But I wanted to go through with the hearing anyway, because more than my fate was at stake: it was a matter of principle. It seemed obvious to me that every one of us has exceptional need when it comes to a matter of life or death. If I could win my case, I hoped it would have a domino effect that benefited other women's cases, other women's desperate appeals. My fund money I had already decided could be used to pay for another woman's course.

I prepared my statistics and arguments carefully before the hearing, though I knew I couldn't win this fight with facts alone. The committee would have to be convinced of my exceptional need for a drug that was not generally available, and they would do that only if placed under an exceptionally strong emotional and moral obligation . . . backed up with the threat of a highly public court battle over human rights.

Still, it helped me to marshal my information. I knew I had to be fully informed because there were heavy economic implications for the trust if they granted my appeal. I was attempting to do something that had never been done before. If I won Herceptin on prescription, I'd be opening the floodgates: across Britain, more than 40,000 women are diagnosed with breast cancer each year. Between a fifth and a quarter of those are HER2 positive, so as many as 10,000 new patients could be candidates for Herceptin annually.

At the end of September, when the Exceptional Needs Committee met, I took Ash's medical documents. The paperwork painted a grim picture of what his life would be like without his mother around to care for him.

The news cameras were rolling as I went into the meeting. A BBC reporter met me at the door and asked how I was feeling. 'Pretty poorly,' I told him. I was suffering from a chest infection, one of the side effects of chemotherapy.

The cameras must have been intimidating for the trust's executives – they were already well aware that this issue was high-profile.

I faced the committee across a table. The committee members looked at me steadily. I wanted to meet their gaze, but the pressure was intense. One of them said, 'You've got ten minutes to state your case,' and I promptly burst into tears.

It has always been difficult for me to talk about Ash without getting emotional and crying. With the stakes so high, it was even tougher. But I managed to get myself under control. I was conscious that I had to be articulate, because I was fighting for all the people who might not be able to say the things I could say. I owed it to them as well as myself.

I said, 'I'm sorry I'm crying, but you've given me ten minutes to fight for my life.'

It was difficult to talk. I swallowed back the tears the whole time I was making my case, but I forced myself to tell them what I'd been through with Ash, and I warned them, 'If that child goes into care, he'll cost the state well in excess of a thousand pounds a week to keep. And I also look after a child with a life-threatening condition who is very seriously ill. Between my role as a parent and my work as a carer, I am a valuable resource both to the health service and the social services.'

The committee expected me, nevertheless, to pay for Herceptin myself. They said, 'You've already got the money. Your fundraising has generated twenty-five thousand pounds in donations. You can afford to fund your own course.'

I said, 'I can, but what about everybody else? There are other women facing desperate choices and this case isn't really just about me, it's the principle. If you give me the drug, I can put the fund to good use, helping other women until the law changes. Because the law has got to change.'

There was no immediate decision. When I walked out of the room, I couldn't be sure I'd won: the tone of the committee was almost offhand. In effect, they said, 'We'll let you know.' In fact, the wheels were turning rapidly. Even the NHS can produce a swift response when it has to. Later that afternoon, I received a phone call.

It was the most significant news of my life. The trust accepted my argument: I could have Herceptin on the grounds of exceptional need.

This was victory. I'd beaten the system. This life-saving drug, the silver bullet that I'd been ready to sell my house to have, that so many people I didn't know had been ready to buy for me, I could now get it on prescription, for nothing.

I wasn't going to be sitting in a hospital car park trying to find a vein so I could administer a dangerous drug to myself. A nurse would see to all that in the comfort and safety of a ward.

I had won.

Exhaustion hit me about half a minute after the euphoria. I was ill, ill, ill. I had a chest infection, I was run down, I had a high temperature. And I thought, I can't go public with this on a Friday afternoon. I needed time to recover before facing more cameras.

I spoke to Alan Carpenter, the head of the PCT, and asked him, 'Please can you keep the news under wraps until Monday morning?'

He said, 'Of course. We just didn't want you to spend the weekend worrying. We'll send you a letter.' That was kind of them. They wanted to go public with it straight away, but they put my needs first. I have to be fair, and emphasise that in the wake of their decision they treated me with great consideration.

The journalists were disappointed. They wanted a statement from me immediately – or, better yet, a blow-by-blow account of the hearing. I was too ill to cope with that right away, so a trade-off was agreed: I promised the news crews that when I opened the PCT's letter on Monday morning, I'd do it in the full glare of their cameras. I didn't tell the reporters I already knew the result, though they suspected. Right through the weekend, they kept calling me. The reporters assumed the PCT was making me wait for the verdict, which reflected badly on the trust.

Monday dawned on a media frenzy. When the television stations are in pursuit of a story, nothing stands in their way – least of all the well-being of the ordinary people whose lives are on display.

Individual reporters do care about you, but they're under so much pressure to produce a story on deadline, they are turned en masse into vultures. So I didn't feel guilty about keeping quiet about the news over the weekend. I told Ash and Richard, but they were sworn to secrecy. We celebrated, but discreetly. On Monday, I tried to look surprised when I opened the letter and read it on television.

I was used to the press by now, of course. They could be ruthless, taking no account of how I was feeling, of whether I'd eaten, or whether I needed to rest. On one day I was filming shortly after a dose of chemo, and I had to run back into the house. A wave of nausea had hit me, and it was no use pretending it would pass.

The camera crew followed me. I was vomiting over the toilet, and they were trying to film me with my head down the bowl. No compassion at all – just an eye for the best television shots. I screamed at them, 'Leave me alone!'

On at least two occasions, I said, 'Please, somebody's got to go out and get me a pasty or something – I've had no food all day.' I didn't have time to cook a meal or even fix myself a sandwich, because the reporters were so relentless. Sky could be unbelievable – they would turn up at half past seven on a Sunday morning, knocking at my door: 'Can you film now?' I had to admire their cheek.

One breakfast programme rang me at half past five one morning and said, 'Good morning! We've got a satellite van outside your house.'

I said, 'Well, they can bloody well go away again. I've got a foster child, I've been up half the night. I don't care if you come back later, but I am not doing it at half past five. My neighbours will complain.' And complain they did, because apparently the outside broadcast unit had been out there since four o'clock that morning with the engine running.

As the news broke that I'd won my battle, the coverage was simply incredible. I was doing television all day on the Monday, and at five o'clock *GMTV* rang me and said,

'Can you get to London? We'll pay for a taxi to bring you up.'

I was exhausted, but *GMTV* had helped me win this fight and I owed them a favour or three. And a day and night in London, at a TV company's expense, would be a great adventure for Ash.

So I left the dog with my neighbour, grabbed Ash and a change of clothing, and we went to London on the spur of the moment. I like to think I'm a fun parent, not a staid parent, so I took him out of school for the day. He doesn't miss a lot of school, but this was too exciting to pass up.

Long before the sun was up, I was putting my make-up on to appear on *GMTV*. As we walked down the hotel corridor to catch our cab, there were newspapers outside all the rooms. And I was on nearly every one. I was unmistakable, in a very distinctive black-and-white-striped outfit. It was surreal to see that suit on almost every front page.

After *GMTV* I had to travel across London to the BBC for the morning news, and then I did Sky. And Channel 4, or Five, after that. The driver eventually dropped us outside the Houses of Parliament, and I said to Ash, 'Let's go on the London Eye.' We had to squeeze in an educational activity or two, and I wasn't in the mood for museums. The London Eye fitted the bill because I was on top of the world.

As we crossed Westminster Bridge, heading for the big wheel, so many people came up to hug me or shake my hand. I'd changed back into my previous day's clothes, the suit with the distinctive black-and-white stripe and the black headscarf – that was all I had to wear. It was a very eye-catching outfit, I was on the front page of every paper, and people were recognising me and coming up to me with congratulations and best wishes. Ash was acting as my mini bodyguard and loving all the excitement: 'Talk to the hand!' he kept saying.

The satisfaction of that moment was beyond words. It felt better than I'd ever dreamed victory could feel.

Chapter Thirteen

My victory started a press frenzy. I always knew it would. 'There's a lot of women out there with exceptional needs,' I told every reporter who called me. 'Everyone has the same right to life.'

It was incredible to find myself part of this furore. The Department of Health was back-pedalling furiously, insisting Somerset Coast's decision did not pave the way for other women to demand treatment. They knew a fifth to a quarter of women diagnosed with breast cancer each year could potentially benefit from Herceptin. That was 10,000 patients who would need a £19,500 course of drugs – as we understood it to cost at the time. Call it £200 million and you wouldn't be far wrong. No wonder they'd fought me so hard.

Emma Taggart, director of policy and campaigns at Breakthrough Breast Cancer, raised another important issue, one that would have a significant impact on budgets: only a third of cancer centres had the equipment to test patients for HER2. Putting that right would be expensive.

But among doctors, there was a huge sense of relief. It must be incredibly frustrating for oncologists to know there's a powerful new drug on the market, one that could deliver a cure to many of their patients, yet be unable to prescribe it.

The *Daily Mail* rang round some of the most prominent doctors in the field, and their reaction was hard-hitting. As I read the quotes, my jaw dropped. In my experience, doctors are cautious. They work all their lives to build their reputations and they don't put anything at risk with reckless words or overstatements.

But here was Dr David Miles, of London Bridge Hospital, declaring, 'Herceptin is one of the biggest advances in the past twenty years. If someone in my family were HER2 positive, I'd go out, buy the drug, put the drip in her arm and administer it myself.'

Professor Ian Smith, professor of cancer medicine at the Royal Marsden, called Herceptin 'a big bang in the breast cancer world, with instantaneous effects [. . .] There is nothing in the world of breast-cancer drugs in the foreseeable future that comes close.'

'We can't afford to wait another twelve months to have Herceptin made available on the NHS,' said Dr Christopher Poole, consultant medical oncologist at Queen Elizabeth Hospital, Birmingham. 'With an aggressive disease, you can't hang around. If there's a delay, women will suffer. If I were a woman with newly diagnosed HER2-positive breast cancer, I'd want Herceptin – and I'd move heaven and earth to get it.'

The consultant medical oncologist at Guy's and St Thomas's Hospital, London, summed up everything I'd been saying for months: 'It's a travesty for this not to be available to the people who need it now.'

I wished I'd had these big guns on my side during my own fight, but I fully recognised how important they would be in the new battle that lay ahead of me – to get Herceptin for every woman who needed it in Britain.

That battle was progressing with dizzying speed. Each day brought new developments, and I was working constantly to keep abreast of the arguments. When journalists phoned me – and my mobile seemed to be ringing constantly – I had the opportunity to publicise the most important information, but I also ran the risk of contradicting myself or getting my facts wrong.

The counterattacks began the same day that my victory was announced, with the Department of Health claiming that NICE could not approve Herceptin because the manufacturer, Roche, had not yet applied for a licence. The drugs giant was still collecting data on the safety implications of using its own product to combat early-stage breast cancer and would not be in a position to submit an application for a licence until February 2006. 'The government cannot dictate when drug companies apply for licences,' said a NICE spokeswoman.

Jeremy Hughes, the chief executive of Breakthrough Breast Cancer, squashed that argument neatly: if Roche had been unable to even put in its application, the procedures were evidently far too complex and time-consuming. 'I would ask why Roche, which published results in the summer, was not in a position to move more quickly,' he said.

A smokescreen of statistics was the government's best defence. The NHS Confederation, which represents health service trusts, did all it could to label my case irrelevant: I had 'exceptional need' and so was not typical of patients.

My situation was a one-off. 'It's misleading to speculate about possible implications for the rest of the NHS,' said Dr Gill Morgan, chief executive of the NHS Confederation. 'The continuing debate about the process by which NICE approves drugs for use in the NHS, and the financial implications of their decisions for NHS trusts, is an entirely separate issue.' To emphasise the government's eagerness to increase budgets for drugs, she pointed out that spending was up by 46 per cent on 2000, at £8 billion a year.

On the back of that, the *Guardian* delivered a personal attack on me and my campaign in a leader article the following day. They didn't just get their facts wrong; they couldn't even spell my name right. 'Barbara Clarke has won a brave battle and given hope to thousands of women suffering from breast cancer,' they admitted. 'But her cause was never as straightforward as her lawyers implied. Indeed, even Solomon might have found reaching a decision difficult.' The arguments my lawyers used had simply been 'wrong', the paper said: Herceptin had not been proved to be safe. 'If people have forgotten Thalidomide, then let them remember Vioxx, a painkiller which had to be withdrawn last year after being linked to 60,000 heart-attack deaths worldwide.'

That made my blood boil. How dare they invoke the spectre of Thalidomide? The drugs were not remotely similar. Herceptin, after all, is designed to prevent the return of a fatal disease, and it is used in conjunction with chemotherapy, which is as toxic an infusion of drugs as the human body can withstand. To put that on a par with a drug that caused horrific defects in pregnancy was shockingly ignorant, a naked attempt to manipulate the emotions of their readers.

And then, just as it seemed the attacks and counter-attacks could not get any more ferocious, Patricia Hewitt turned up the heat. On 5 October 2005, she announced all patients with early-stage breast cancer would be tested to see if their tumours were HER2 positive and they could benefit from Herceptin. 'This drug has the potential to save many women's lives and I want to see it in widespread use on the NHS,' she insisted.

The cancer charity BACUP underlined the importance of the announcement: currently, only half of patients were tested at diagnosis, said the chief executive, Joanna Rule, and a quarter were not tested at all. 'This is extremely good news,' she said. 'An automatic right to a HER2 test will allow women to know what their treatment options are, so this is an important step in the right direction.'

I was equally enthusiastic, though I emphasised there was still a long way to go. 'It will offer a lifeline to many women suffering with breast cancer,' I told reporters. 'Although today's decision is to be welcomed, what about the women in between? Of the women that were diagnosed before the government's decision today, there will be about a thousand who will die before the drug is made available.'

Not everyone welcomed the news. Joe Collier, a professor of medicines policy at St George's Hospital Medical School, London, lashed out at Patricia Hewitt: 'It is unacceptable that the minister should be pressurising the licensing authority or dictating to NICE about the proper use of medicines. What they should certainly do is make sure the decision by NICE is very fast. That would be reasonable. But this is a dangerous precedent and Patricia Hewitt should back off.'

The debate moved on like a rollercoaster. The following day, the *Guardian*'s health editor, Sarah Bosely, reported that UK cancer care was almost the worst in Europe, according to figures presented to the European Parliament by a research group of Swedish economists. I was staggered to learn that the Czech Republic, Hungary and Poland all matched our standards, while most other countries easily exceeded them. Where cancer was concerned, the NHS might as well have been an Eastern European bureaucracy. The Karolinska Institute laid the blame squarely on NICE. To back up the research, figures from Columbia University in New York proved, unsurprisingly, that where patients had faster access to new treatments, survival rates were higher.

And yet the prognosis did not have to be bleak. Cancer was no longer the automatic death sentence it had once been. Professor Michel Coleman of Cancer Research UK produced analysis based on a decade of statistics: since 1995 more than 400,000 people had been diagnosed with breast cancer. Two-thirds of women who had discovered lumps between 2001 and 2003 could hope to survive twenty years, up from just over half from the period between 1996 and 1998. 'Overall long-term survival for women with breast cancer has improved dramatically over the past ten years and we are seeing even better survival statistics for women in their fifties and sixties,' he said. He was alarmed, though, by the UK's poor performance in comparison with our neighbours. 'We need to catch up further with Western Europe. Other countries that are doing particularly well include the Nordic countries, Switzerland and France. They have higher survival rates partly due to earlier diagnosis.'

Tony Howell, Cancer Research UK's consultant medical oncologist at the Christie Hospital in Manchester, hailed the report: 'In the clinic we can say you have more chance of dying from something else than you have of dying from your breast cancer.'

The head of policy at Breakthrough Breast Cancer, Sarah Rawlings, was even more optimistic: 'Ultimately what we would really like to see is breast cancer becoming a preventable disease.'

These were the headiest days I'd ever experienced. It is almost impossible to convey how completely the situation was reversed from my despair just six months earlier. Then, I had been waiting to die. Now, I was part of a campaign machine with the declared objective of making breast cancer a disease of the past.

And in the midst of this, I had my first dose of Herceptin. Before I could take advantage of the PCT's verdict, I finished my course of chemo. I heard I'd won on 30 September, and the Herceptin treatment started around the middle of October. By then I was also undergoing radiotherapy at Bristol Oncology Centre.

Radiotherapy was gruelling. My home was fifty miles from Bristol Oncology Centre, and on the crowded M5 the journey, in a Red Cross car, could easily take an hour and a half. The treatment itself took only a few minutes, and sometimes I was seen immediately, but on other occasions

I might have to wait for two hours or longer. Then I had to travel home, only to do it again the next day . . . and the next. That went on for five weeks, five days a week, and inevitably part of the treatment fell during the school holidays. It was too much to ask Ash to cope with all that travelling, so for part of the time we stayed at the centre – that's no place for a child, because it is traumatic for a young mind to witness so much illness. Many of the people there were seriously ill, and we could read the pain and fear in their faces. But we had no choice, and Ash bravely and patiently passed hours in the waiting room. Afterwards, to brighten his day, we would visit the SS *Great Britain*, Brunel's Clifton Suspension Bridge or At-Bristol, which was great fun but terribly tiring in the middle of radiotherapy.

As part of the treatment, four or five spots were tattooed on to my breasts. They will be with me for the rest of my life, a permanent reminder of the ordeal. They look like dirty marks and I suggested to the nurses how much better it would be if they used a semi-permanent dye, which would eventually fade. I am able to accept the marks, but for some women they must be heartbreaking.

There was no time to have Herceptin at home, so the first dose was administered at the Bristol Oncology Centre.

It was important to maintain public awareness and ensure that this wasn't a nine-day wonder that slid off the schedules, so I remembered my old brainwave and decided I wanted to be administered Herceptin in front of the news cameras. The centre's staff were reluctant, and refused to allow a crew inside. Undeterred, I hatched a plot. I asked the doctors if it would be all right for me to take a camcorder into the centre.

They said, 'If you want to film yourself, we can't stop you – so long as you don't film anybody else.'

I took one of the journalists, Helen Callaghan, in with me. She had become a friend, and that was how I introduced her, but I did neglect to mention that she was also a reporter. So the first time I had Herceptin I was on camera, looking ill and frightened: I was very aware of the one in 200 risk of serious heart problems. I always seem to over-react to drugs, anyway – I'm the sort of person who gets hopelessly drunk on one glass of wine. I kept smiling for the camera, but I was terrified.

Before I left the house, I'd put my will and power of attorney on the kitchen table, and made arrangements for Ash to go to Gina's after school – in case I wasn't allowed home, but also because of the small but real possibility that something would go wrong.

In the end, that first dose took six hours, though these days it's over in two. My blood pressure dropped, probably because of anxiety and the stress I was under. The footage was fairly dramatic. I was supposed to be filming myself, but at one point the camcorder started to travel round the room. My friends were ringing me afterwards, to ask, 'How did you manage that?' It must have been strange for them to watch.

To win my fight, I was having to be very vocal and public, yet I'm actually a private person. Uri told me, 'Everybody wants to be famous,' but I don't. I'd hate to be as famous as Uri Geller. He loves it; he doesn't even mind negative publicity. I don't like being in the limelight, but sometimes to save your life you have to make exceptions. And I had managed to do it. What I couldn't help thinking of, though, were all the women who weren't in a position to sell their houses or run a publicity campaign but who had just as much right as me to Herceptin. I knew that I had to help them.

Chapter Fourteen

By the time my Herceptin treatment had started, my Herceptin Treatment Fund stood at just over £25,000, and more fundraising was planned. That money was a heavy responsibility. I had to use it to save as many lives as possible.

Originally, I'd thought I would use all of the money I had raised to pay for the treatment of one woman. But my private consultant, Dr Hassan, rang me. 'Please don't do that,' he urged. 'Please offer everybody one dose, because there are so many women who are self-funding or who want to self-fund. You can help fifteen women instead of just one.'

So that's what I did.

The young woman I gave the first donation to was an office worker. She was one of those who simply could not do publicity. The press would love her, but she couldn't face it. She was only twenty-nine, recently married, and had lost her breast. She felt unable to face having her name in the press.

Her health authority felt she didn't have exceptional circumstances – she didn't have a child. She didn't earn a great deal of money, and my heart went out to her.

I can understand what motivates people like Ian Liddell-Grainger because the stories that ordinary people have to tell can make me fume. This young woman didn't want to stage sleep-ins, fight her local trust all the way to the Court of Appeal, campaign on radio and television, or even tell her friends that she was ill. Even when I begged her – 'Go public with me, please, to help other women' – she couldn't do it.

She said, 'Your argument is very strong, but there's no way. I can't face the press. It would kill me.' Who would dare to say that she had less right to life than anyone else with cancer?

I believed she had every right to be looking forward to life – planning a family, making progress in her career, buying her first home with her new husband. Her life should have been ahead of her, but part of her died the day they told her she couldn't have the drug that could save her.

She was penalised, too, by the postcode lottery, the non-sensical system that in effect means that the healthcare we receive depends on where we live. If she had been registered in Devon or Cornwall, Herceptin would have been available to her on NHS prescription from the end of October 2005. The eleven trusts that covered those counties and the Scilly Isles, under the umbrella of the South West Peninsula Strategic Health Authority, had agreed the drug should be made available immediately to all patients without a licence from NICE, at a predicted annual cost of £4 million. There were two conditions: the treatment had to be backed by the patient's doctors and the patient had to understand the medicine had not yet been fully tested. A Roche spokesman said a 3,000-page dossier had been compiled to support their application for a licence, but it could take NICE nine months to weigh it up.

A few miles north of Devon, a south Somerset district councillor, Mrs Linda Vijeh, was being forced to sell her house to pay for care at a private clinic in India. Fearing cancer would kill her if she waited, she was flying to Pune for a month-long treatment. She told reporters, 'It takes some leap of faith to fly to a Third World country to be operated on by a doctor you have never met, in a hospital you've never heard of. But that is how desperate I was.' I knew how she felt: I'd faced the same choices.

Around this time, I learned of ten women in Swindon fighting to get the drug: the statistics suggested that in the course of the next twelve months, cancer would come back in two cases. With Herceptin, it would only come back in one.

So within a year, at least one of those women could be saved from a death sentence. One in ten: that's a terrifying ratio. And if you were one of those ten, you would be fighting tooth and nail for your life.

One of the women needed her first dose of Herceptin immediately, and I decided to support her through my fund. I had to. Her PCT took so long to answer her letter she didn't have enough time to take her case to court. The legal process could have taken months, and that was time she didn't have.

My fund was a very simple set-up. It paid for one dose of Herceptin for people who were self-funding, and it wasn't usually the first dose. I started off paying for the first dose, which was £2,500, with subsequent doses at around £1,200 to £1,500. Later, I realised that to help as many women as possible who were self-funding, I could help the maximum number of people by paying for one of the later doses for each of them. I was able to donate £11,500 to the Dorothy Griffiths Breast Cancer Appeal Fund, to help treat six women in Stoke-on-Trent.

In the Swindon case, I had to pay for the first dose. The woman could then carry on fundraising for the next one. She needed it right away, and it was no good telling her to raise that much money by the end of the week because she wouldn't be able to.

Patricia Hewitt continued to pile pressure on the trusts. On 25 October, she issued guidelines forbidding them to withhold the drug on grounds of cost alone. Accepting that there would have to be trade-offs within hospital budgets to pay for courses of Herceptin, she cited 'huge frustration' among patients. When a mother of four, forty-one-year-old Elaine Barber of Staffordshire, threatened to take North Stoke Primary Care Trust to the High Court, the health secretary demanded to see the evidence behind the trust's ruling that she should be denied Herceptin. The PCT spokesman said, 'The evidence of this drug as a cost-effective use of finite health resources is not confirmed. It would therefore be premature to introduce it as a routine treatment.'

Elaine told reporters, 'I cannot believe that my life is being measured in pounds. I've been put through all this just so the health authority can balance the books.'

A day later, the PCT crumbled and the decision was reversed. The health secretary was pulling no punches. 'I accept that some PCTs are already under financial pressure,' she said, 'and they may have to make difficult trade-offs in priorities to fund this new treatment for women who want it and whose clinicians want it for them. Though that will not be easy, I believe it is the right thing to do, particularly as they will be managing it over two financial years.'

What made Patricia Hewitt's intervention more important still was that the medical research continued to demonstrate that Herceptin was no ordinary drug. Its results were close to miraculous. Trials published in the *New England Journal of Medicine* showed recurrence rates could be cut by 46 per cent. Dr Richard Gelber of Harvard's Dana Carver Cancer Institute said, 'This is probably the biggest evidence of a treatment effect I've ever seen in oncology. It is quite remarkable.'

Doctors were still divided about exactly what was causing such a dramatic effect. In theory, Herceptin was blocking the growth of tumours by binding itself to the receptors on HER2-positive cancer cells, to stop them from dividing and multiplying. However, some medics believed the drug was stimulating the natural human immune system to fight off the cancer, or perhaps, in tandem with the chemotherapy cocktail, simply obliterating the HER2 cells.

As the beginning of November arrived, the annual Bridgwater Carnival supplied another opportunity to generate funds. The floats wind their way through the town, and the whole course is a long walk. I was finding the radiotherapy exhausting, and doing this walk was going to be a major challenge. One of the effects of Herceptin was to make me breathless. But if I started making excuses, I'd be letting down every woman with cancer in the country, including myself.

I had quite a lot of trouble getting anybody to walk with me. Of the other local women with cancer, none felt well enough to join me. I thought, I know I can do it. It's going to be tiring, but I am going to do it.

So I got myself an Elizabeth I costume and dressed up Ash as a dinosaur. Paul, Alison and Scott came as Fagin, Nancy and Oliver, and a couple of my other friends came with stripy jumpers and strings of onions, greeting everyone with cries of ''Allo, 'allo!' One of them had been through breast cancer herself. They run the local French jive class and they danced all the way through the carnival.

The local radio station joined us, all in pink wigs, and another friend, Alison, came as a witch. Marching together, we went out with our collecting pots. We were allowed to keep half the money for the Herceptin Treatment Fund – the other half went to the Bridgwater Carnival pool of charity funds. I filled about four of these pots, because I was quite determined.

It was pouring. I had false breasts on because I needed a bigger bust for the costume. The only bit of me that was dry was under the two plastic cones. I was squelching. My royal robes soaked up puddles to the waist in the pouring rain. I couldn't even see properly for the rain, since my eyelashes were missing, but I smiled the whole way through, and I was amazed by the number of people still there at the end. They were laughing and smiling, too, standing there looking bedraggled but happy, watching the carnival. I bounced through it, and when I finally peeled my costume off in my bathroom, I had big red marks across my legs where the wet fabric had flopped.

Ash's dinosaur costume was made of foam and also soaked up the rain. And we managed to lose our neighbours' two twelve-year-old children – I thought they were with my brother, but they'd wandered off, so at the end of the carnival I had to walk back into town. One of my neighbours received a phone call from the town hall to tell us they'd found these two young girls. They must have just dashed off right at the beginning, when it was all very exciting. But we made some good money, and my neighbours were very forgiving. The moral of this tale is, don't trust me with your children.

I don't mind being a well-known face around Bridgwater. Everybody comes up to me with a smile, though there are a few exceptions. One man approached me in the vet's once and said, 'I don't see why you should get the drug and everybody else shouldn't.'

I said, 'That's why I'm carrying on fighting for everyone else. I agree with you, it's not right.'

His wife said, 'You don't read the newspapers, do you,' and she told him off.

But he wouldn't let it go: 'You shouldn't get it just because you're a nurse,' he said. So he obviously didn't understand anything about where I was coming from.

More distressing were the pieces of hate mail that dropped through my letterbox. The vast majority of the letters and emails I received were positive and uplifting – there were a few, though, that were thoroughly poisonous. 'You must have sinned against God to get cancer,' wrote one correspondent.

People had also gone to quite some effort to send some horrendous racism, which shows how sick they were. Fortunately, Ash has the most sunny disposition and he copes very well with racism. It just bounces off him. He makes a joke of it.

Richard is much more reserved. He doesn't respond at all to name-calling; he just ignores it. Racism is beneath his notice. 'They are small-minded, ignorant people,' he once told me, 'and I won't react to it.' Richard is a very serious, sincere and deep young man.

I called a friend on the *Express* to ask advice. She told me, 'I get three letters like that every week. I bet they didn't put their name on it. If you appear in the newspapers, you attract people like that.'

My first reaction was to be shocked and distressed, but the journalist's practical viewpoint helped me put the incident in perspective: this was more than an outburst of anger and hatred. The senders must have mental-health problems. No one in a rational state of mind could send such filth. I had to understand that it wasn't personal, that these people did have a problem – and it was their problem and not mine.

In one instance, however, I had to go to the police and ask them to act. Halfway through my chemotherapy, I had started to receive distressing messages: 'I hope you die in pain.' I was very ill, and I knew I might soon die. Those messages started to play on my mind. I should not have let them get to me; I ought to have been able to put them to the back of my mind. They were meaningless noise, but they upset me. It was as if, while my friends were praying for me, someone was out there cursing me violently. The police held off for about ten days because they thought at first it wouldn't be helpful for them to intervene, but eventually they served the sender with a harassment order. The letters stopped immediately.

Chapter Fifteen

By late October, I was feeling frustrated at the slowness of the government's progress and was again searching for ways to keep the pressure on. Once my course of Herceptin had started, I no longer had the threat of taking on the NHS in the Human Rights Court, which was a good thing for me personally but not much help to the thousands of other women waiting for the drug.

So I rang the health secretary's office and told her PA, 'I would really like to speak to Ms Hewitt. I'm a campaigner and I want to say thank you.'

Most ministers don't receive many calls from campaigners who want to offer thanks. The PA sounded a bit shocked, and I pressed my advantage: 'Ms Hewitt is getting a lot of criticism in the papers at the moment and I think it's undeserved. She has saved the lives of a great many women in this country by taking the flak.'

At half past nine one evening, she called and offered to sponsor me and Ash for the entire length of the Bridgwater Carnival parade. I thanked her for putting pressure on NICE, and she said, 'Well, it's not me, it's you that's done everything.' So we had a little mutual-admiration session, showering each other in praise.

I said, 'I couldn't have done it without you, because when

you went public and said Herceptin didn't need to be licensed or approved by NICE before it could be prescribed, that swung it for me. So thank you.'

'No, no, thank you.'

'No, no, no, thank you.'

Then we both burst out laughing. I had the immediate impression this was a genuine person who had retained her humour and sense of perspective. She was straightforward, explaining what she could do and what was beyond her power, and, during the course of our long conversation, I saw that she had her back up against the wall. In a world where she was trying to change things, she actually had less power than she needed. People assume that as a senior minister, she's all-powerful. After talking with her, I understood that's not so.

Let me be absolutely plain about this: the National Health Service is one of Britain's flagship institutions. It's this country at its best. And that's why, when it fails to do its job properly, everyone from Land's End to John o'Groats should be up in arms. You don't have to be a patient to feel passionate about the NHS. Patricia Hewitt has been a good health secretary because she believes that fervently.

Throughout my campaign, one of my biggest fears was that I might in some way damage the health service. I don't want to criticise – I want to improve. There are areas where the health service is falling well below its own high standards, and cancer care is one of them. Had I known that years ago, even if I hadn't suffered from cancer, I would have fought, because the health service matters to me. I've devoted my career to nursing, and I've always been on the side of the underdog.

But I didn't realise, and it's not obvious until you actually start to research it yourself, that there's a double standard in medical care. We all know that people can jump the queue by opting to go private, but I thought that was the limit of the unfairness. I didn't realise there were life-saving treatments that were available only if you went privately.

It's common knowledge that if you want a hip operation you can jump the queue. That's what you pay for. I didn't know you could pay to save your life.

So I had this genuine fear that the whole health service was going to be plunged into crisis because I was jumping up and down about these extremely expensive drugs. The publicity my case generated was so intense, and the warnings from the NHS economists were so dire, that it sometimes seemed a real possibility. That was never my intention: I wanted to save lives, not play politics. And these lives were very real – it wasn't just statistics on a sheet of paper.

When healthcare and politics combine, the complexities are mind-boggling. Why couldn't the trusts let women purchase Herceptin from them at cost price? There's no excuse. But as long as it could not be prescribed by the NHS, they would not sell it back to us at their reduced rate. Before I was diagnosed with cancer, I had no idea about this labyrinth. I knew that there were funding difficulties in certain areas, but I had no idea that British cancer care was literally on a par with Lithuania. That's entirely down to funding, and NICE. Originally, NICE was put in place to end the postcode lottery, but it hasn't done that. Instead, it became a cost-cutting exercise. While NICE sits on a drug for five years and decides whether it's safe or not, that's five years of funding that doesn't have to be found. Meanwhile the rest of Europe is getting the latest and best treatments.

I think this situation has probably gone on for years, but even as a nurse I hadn't known about it because I'd never worked in cancer care. Now that I have had an opportunity to see at first hand how desperate the situation is, I have been forced to re-evaluate some of my opinions.

I have never thought of myself as political, and I would not want to be a politician – that world moves too slowly for my patience. But when I first asked my NHS consultant for Herceptin and was turned down, I told him I would take my fight as far as I had to – even to the House of Commons. He said, 'Oh, don't go getting all political on me.'

I snapped, 'It absolutely is political. You can't say I shouldn't get political, because this is politics. When my life isn't worth saving, that is politics.'

It's all about financial costs weighed against human costs. At the end of November 2005, opponents of Herceptin found the ammunition they were looking for, in the medical journal *Annals of Oncology*. It reported healthcare systems across Europe could be placed under intolerable pressure because of the high cost of HER2 drugs, and warned that other budgets would have to be slashed to compensate. A health economist at Belgium's Ghent University named Mattias Neyt calculated that the use of Herceptin was likely to double as it was extended to women with early-stage breast cancer. I couldn't understand his logic – after all, if growths are caught at the early stage, they don't develop into late-stage breast cancer and therefore don't require ongoing treatment with Herceptin. It seems a desirable trade-off to me: buy a six-month course for two women and at least one of them will not require a five-year course at a later date. *Annals of Oncology*, however, warned that Herceptin was going to inflict a £107-million burden on the NHS. 'Countries should not rush into prescribing it before working out the implications very carefully and being prepared to reallocate resources, get rid of other treatments that are no longer effective and drive a hard bargain over the price of the drug,' the report said.

Within ten days, another set of astounding trial results was pressing the human value of the drug. An American-led study, involving more than 3,000 patients from forty-three countries, showed the rate of recurrence in early-stage breast cancer could be cut by 51 per cent. Dr Andrew Wardley of the Christie Hospital in Manchester was in no doubt: 'These results confirm the outstanding benefit of Herceptin in early breast cancer and make it imperative that all breast cancers are tested for HER2 status at diagnosis and appropriate patients receive Herceptin.'

If there have to be cutbacks in other areas, I want to know what can be more important than a treatment that's proven to increase survival rates by more than half. I believe this so passionately that I am willing to risk upsetting a minority of people by voicing some controversial views. The NHS funds operations that I regard as non-essential, such as sex-change operations and certain plastic-surgery procedures. What about keeping people alive? We all pay into the system first and foremost to be kept alive and to have quality of life, and I feel that a lot of money is going to the wrong places. People have rung me up and challenged my views on this, asking, 'What about people who need hip replacements?' I'm not saying people shouldn't have new hips when they need them, but the PCTs do need to look carefully at their budgets to find the wasted cash, money that often vanishes without trace. They urgently need to look at the closure and reopening of wards, the redecoration, the funding of art – all these wastes of valuable resources. No NHS money should be spent on art. In Taunton, the PCT asks for art to be donated or sponsored by local businesses. That's the right thing to do. It explains why Taunton isn't in a mess with money: it's a well-run trust. For instance, it tries not to employ agency nurses. The trust has a bank of staff because agency doctors and nurses cost health authorities a fortune.

The crisis in the NHS comes down to mismanagement of money. During our phone conversation, Patricia Hewitt emphasised to me that she doesn't have an endless pot that the government can keep filling up with money. The health authorities seriously mismanage their money. They waste it. There's no other word for it. Look abroad – Germany makes its health system work on a tighter budget. And efficiency varies wildly from one region of the UK to another. If one trust can make its funding work, why can't another? It's not all down to the catchment area. Mismanagement is much more complicated than that. The PCTs have got to be able to balance their books. And they mustn't do that by cutting back on care that can save lives.

And that's why I completely support Patricia Hewitt, even when she's being booed and slow-clapped at a nurses' convention. I'm a nurse, and the nurses are quite right to protest at cutbacks that take their jobs away. I hate to see nursing staff being cut. Nurses are under immense pressure, but the real point is that NHS money is being wasted.

I saw it when I was nursing in hospitals. In the early days of HIV, we had considerable budgets to spend, and if you didn't spend your budget, you lost it for the next year. In the end, my department bought furniture and lighting, and they bought it in a hurry because they had to spend the money by the close of the year. It turned out to be totally unsuitable for our needs, so all that money was wasted. It was stupid.

We should have been able to say, 'We don't want to spend the budget this year, but we will need it next year,' or, 'Let it go to a unit that does need it immediately.' But the health service doesn't work that way – you have to spend it within a deadline.

That kind of waste happens right across the NHS. I saw it with Bristol's Frenchay Hospital, which was scheduled for closure: the PCT put a colossal amount of money into doing that building up. Surely somebody had an inkling that it might be closing? Why put millions into renovations and refurbishment?

In one county where I worked, the health authority employed a financial analyst to come in and he got them into worse trouble. They paid him a fortune, but he couldn't find the lost money. Instead, he advised unworkable cutbacks.

So what do health authorities do to balance the books? They sack nurses. I've worked on the wards and I know they are invariably short-staffed. Those nurses are exhausted. That's not who we should be getting rid of. It's not even as if our nurses are well paid. By sacking a nurse, the PCT saves next to nothing. Our doctors, on the other hand, earn a lot more than the doctors in Germany. But does anyone have the courage to address that issue?

One solution might be for the PCTs to employ more practice nurses, because they are now able to issue prescriptions in surgeries. I've known many nurses who were more experienced than their doctors, better able to sum up a situation and identify the necessary treatment, because they were the ones getting hands-on experience day and night.

Working on the wards is absolutely exhausting. I've worked on care of the elderly wards where I was told I had three or four people to get ready in the morning, all of them very dependent, and then I would discover I actually had seven or eight people under my care. One would be calling for a bed pan, another might be trying to wander down to breakfast in a pyjama top. It was a terrific strain to provide adequate care, but if I ever said as much, there would be a black mark against my name. The administrators would assume I couldn't cope, and I'm the most 'coping' person around. A lot of nurses won't complain because they don't want to have those fatal words said about them: 'She's not coping.' They know they are under-staffed, but they labour on silently. It is happening throughout wards up and down the country – people are not standing up and saying, 'This ward is unsafe with so few staff on it.'

To make matters worse, the paperwork is horrendous and it has to be done – patients don't require less care just because the sister has a sheaf of forms to fill in. When I worked in Hastings as a school nurse doing a lot of child protection, I repeatedly said that I was overworked. I'd tell my manager, 'Look, I'm taking work home at night, and the last nurse who was here before me was two years behind in her work. I'm slaving into the early hours on my paper-work to keep up with it.'

The response was, 'Aren't you coping, Barbara?' The tone would be caring, but I'd know exactly what was meant.

I'd be assertive with them: 'I am really capable of coping, believe me. But I'm having to take a lot of work home and I am just letting you know that.'

Nothing was done, but when I left, the managers had to hire two people to cope with the workload!

I come from a culture of not complaining, because nurses never do, and that made it doubly difficult for me to become a campaigner. I saw myself as a foot soldier, not a general. I think I always expected there to be somebody else who would make it right. But in fact it's up to all of us. We foot the bill – we should make it our business to care where the money goes.

If people were told that by putting an extra pound a week into their health service, it would improve beyond imagination, I am sure they would understand why their contributions had gone up. Except of course, at the moment, if we put in an extra pound a week it would probably go on furniture and art – or computer software that doesn't work.

Britain's health service belongs to all of us. It isn't the property of the accountants and the civil servants – ordinary people pay for it, and ordinary people have to take responsibility for it.

As the political fighting intensified in the Herceptin campaign during November, I was determined to do all I could. I might have been tired to the bone, but I wasn't going to rest.

Chapter Sixteen

My cancer had happened with perfect timing. When I discovered the lump, it was too early for me to have Herceptin on the NHS – and I had ended up changing government policy. I was playing my part in making a life-saving drug available five years sooner than scheduled, which meant 9,000 lives would be saved. That was an astonishing, empowering feeling.

'I don't consider cancer a blight on my life,' I said to Sarah Boobyer, the *Mercury* reporter. 'It has been a blessing and I can now look back on those dark days and feel I know the reason I had it. The day I was told I had breast cancer was the worst day of my life, and I kept asking myself, Why me? Well, now I know why.'

My phone was still ringing off the hook. During my interview with Sarah, a television company contacted me, and a magazine journalist called to ask if I could feature in their Christmas special. I can only remember those details because Sarah faithfully recorded them. She has been my tireless supporter, and I was so thrilled for her when she won a national award in recognition of her work. Newsquest named her Highly Commended Runner-Up in the Scoop of the Year category – an incredible achievement for a reporter on a weekly paper.

A week before Christmas, I had my first all-clear. It was no more than a check-up, because the full mammogram wasn't due until February, but when the doctors said they couldn't see any sign of cancer, and that I appeared to be in remission, I was so relieved. I had been through so many gruelling treatments to reach this point. Sometimes it felt as if the cures were killing me, and I had needed all my resolve to keep believing that I was going to come out healthy on the other side of the ordeal. Now I was hearing the news I'd dreamed of every day. It was like emerging into sunlight.

That same week, a mother of two in Swindon won the right to challenge her local health authority in the High Court after they ruled she could not have Herceptin on prescription. Her name was Ann Marie Rogers, and she had borrowed £5,000 to have the first two doses of the drug privately. The judge, Mr Justice Charles, ruled that her case had at least enough merit to be heard in full: this didn't mean she was going to win her fight, but it did mean the health authority could not completely ignore her. They had to face her, and her lawyer, the leading solicitor Yogi Amin, in the High Court.

Better still, the judge ordered Swindon PCT to continue with Ann Marie's treatment until the hearing in February. That meant the Herceptin course recommended by her doctor would not be interrupted, and that she could hope to have the whole course funded by the NHS if she won her case in February. 'I'm thrilled with the result,' she said. 'It has made my Christmas.' It made Christmas, too, for a great many women who knew that if the courts ordered the PCT to treat Ann Marie with Herceptin, other trusts up and down the country would have little choice but to fall in line.

As soon as I read about Ann Marie's case, I phoned her solicitor and arranged for us to be put in touch. 'I have been saying for weeks that somebody needs to go to court, to press the human-rights issue,' I told her. 'It can't be me, because my personal need for Herceptin has been resolved. But this is about far more than any one person. You are the first patient to make a case who is entitled to legal aid. It's essential that you use that advantage and fight your PCT in the courts.'

I had other bonuses to look forward to that Christmas. Most important of all was the knowledge that this was much less likely to be my last. There had been a bleak time, only months earlier, when I truly thought that Ash, Richard and I would only have a few more Christmases together. Instead, my strength was returning and my spirits were high. It was the best gift I could have imagined. And there were other surprise presents, such as the nominations from dozens of strangers across the country who voted for me to be Tesco Mum of the Year.

The presentation took place at the Waldorf Hilton on the Strand, in London, shortly after New Year. Richard and Ash both wore new suits for the occasion: Ash had a sharp and stylish outfit that we bought on eBay, but the biggest surprise was seeing Richard in a suit. I thought I would be lucky to coax him into a jacket and tie, but he told me, 'I'm going to look my best because I'm proud of you.' That made my eyes brim with tears.

My award was presented to me by the actress Rita

Tushingham. I'd been a fan for a long time, because I remembered her from 1960s classics like *A Taste of Honey*. Rita told me her daughter, Aisha, who was thirty-three, had also been diagnosed with breast cancer: she was fully informed about the state of cancer care within the NHS. When I was called to the stage to collect my Special Recognition Award, I was delighted to also receive a massive bouquet. It was twenty minutes before I spotted the envelope nestling in the blooms and opened it to discover £1,000 of Cosmos holiday vouchers.

Ash was asked to make a short speech. 'Mum,' he said, 'you are amazing. Because of you more children like me get to spend more time with their mums. I love you.'

The award ceremony took place in January 2006 and I hadn't yet told Richard or Ash about my first, tentative all-clear in December. There was a high risk that the cancer might return soon, and I didn't want to raise the boys' hopes only to dash them. After my mammogram at the end of February, however, I could no longer see any need to hide the good news. It seemed unfair to make them wait years for the definitive statement that I was officially in remission – especially as even that declaration could give no guarantees that I would always be free from cancer. If I was optimistic, the boys deserved to share that feeling, and I phoned Richard from the car as soon as I walked out of the hospital. He was at work, and he was almost speechless with relief. 'I've been so desperately worried about you, Mum,' he said at last.

A camera crew had been in contact with me earlier in the day, and they called to hear the news. I explained that I was on my way home to tell Ash, who would soon be home from school. The journalists asked, quite gently and respectfully, whether they could be on hand to witness the moment when I told Ash that I'd had the all-clear. I knew Ash would appreciate that, so I invited them to the house. When Ash walked in, I gave him a huge hug and said, 'I've got something fantastic to tell you. I went to the doctor's today and they took a good look at me and said that the lump has gone. Completely gone. Mummy's clear of cancer.'

I choked up and couldn't say any more. I didn't need to. Ash squeezed me and wouldn't let go, and I clung to him. Later, I was glad we'd shared the moment with the cameras, because a stream of calls and emails told me that many other people had been moved and inspired by it.

The news that I was officially in remission promptly put me on the *Daily Mirror*'s front page, under the banner heading 'Wonder Woman', announcing a 'cure'. I was curled up with embarrassment. The next thing I knew, an irate woman from *Nursing Standard* was on the phone. 'How could you go public with this?' she demanded. 'It's not helpful to other breast-cancer sufferers.'

But I hadn't told anyone I was 'cured'. I'm a nurse: of course I understand that remission isn't a cure. Editors hate to leave a running story unfinished. They want closure, and happy endings sell papers. It doesn't matter whether they're writing about an unknown woman from Bridgwater or Kylie Minogue – they want to tell their readers that we're 'cured of cancer'.

It was as though my story had taken on a life of its own.

It was wonderful news, but there was a big contrast with the way I really felt – tired and fragile, frightened that a new lump could appear at any time and daunted by the knowledge that I would have to remain in remission for years before I could truly be considered cancer-free.

I spent the rest of the day in front of the TV cameras explaining it was far too early to be sure about remission. 'I'm still facing a fifty per cent chance that the cancer will come back this year. It's like tossing a coin every day of my life. But unfortunately, fighting so hard for a drug doesn't buy you immunity from the disease. So when people say, "Of course, it's worked for you," I have to be honest and tell them, "Only so far."'

I was, however, full of hope, and intensely grateful to everyone who had helped me to stay alive. By the time I was officially in remission, I knew I'd had several months with Ash and Richard that I wouldn't have otherwise had. After my operation, I had been told that the growth would almost certainly be back in four to seven months, if I didn't have Herceptin.

Shortly after this, the *Sun* invited me to their Wonder Mum Awards, and I went along with Gina, her daughter and Ash. I wanted to bring Gina because she had been so kind and supportive. Sharon Osbourne was the host, and meeting her was a pleasure – she looked straight at me and said, 'You go, girl!' And it was fun to meet Trinny and Susannah, from *What Not to Wear* . . . even if they did comment on my 'chunky calves'.

Before the ceremony at the Savoy in London, I had my photograph taken with Trinny and Susannah and they said,

'Barbara, you look lovely, you're absolutely appropriately dressed.'

I'm afraid that made me a little too confident. I went over to their table later and said, 'Would you mind, girls, giving me some advice? I've got these shiny tights on and I don't think they do anything for me.'

'OK, lift up your skirt. Oh my God, chunky calves! Stay away from shiny tights – bare legs or matt!' they shrieked in unison.

'Thank you so much, girls,' I said. I'd stuck my head in the lion's mouth, so I deserved whatever I got. But they were so funny I couldn't ever take offence. They're a comedy team. I binned the tights, though.

Stockings were more in keeping with my style, because I had adopted a forties look. It was the headscarves that did it. I thought, I can either go ethnic and do the African thing with headscarves or I can go forties. I began to buy seamed stockings on the Internet, which almost provoked heart attacks in one or two cameramen. 'Oh my God,' one chap gasped, 'you've got seamed stockings – are they silk?'

I said, 'No, they're fully-fashioned nylons.' The poor man nearly dropped dead on the spot.

I did the same thing to Des Lynam, at the Wonder Mum Awards. Des was with a rather attractive lady, and I asked him, 'Is this your wife?'

He said, 'No, she's my agent. I'm not married.'

I said, 'Oh, Des, would you marry me?'

He said, 'Why?'

I said, 'I want to be the envy of middle-aged women everywhere.'

We laughed and started talking about my retro look. He said I looked very fifties today, because I had a fifties frock on, and I said that when I'd gone for the forties look I'd done it right down to the seamed stockings. I said, 'You look like the sort of man who wouldn't mind getting on his knees and straightening my seams.'

I honestly thought he was going to have a coronary. I have never seen anyone blush as much as Des Lynam did. He laughed and laughed, and at last he said, 'Well, you are a very interesting companion for lunch. I'm afraid I'm going to have to turn you down on the marriage offer, but I'm going to tell all my friends that Barbara Clark proposed to me and she wears seamed stockings.'

Uri chaperoned me to the Wonder Mum Awards. He was brilliant. He's just such a character, I love him to bits, even though he can't keep a secret – you can't tell him anything. But he's adorable and very loyal: he's my friend and I think a lot of him.

He pointed out all the celebs to me – Nell McAndrew, Joe Swash from *EastEnders*, Melinda Messenger, Julia Haworth from *Coronation Street* and *Emmerdale*'s Matthew Bose.

'You're a bigger star than anyone here,' Uri told me sweetly.

You can't take him seriously. 'Would you like my autograph?' I said.

Uri and Ash were cheering when I went up on stage to collect my award from G4, the 'popera' group. And we were all cheering when the main prize, a year's free shopping at a supermarket chain, was given to a lady called Brenda

Benfield, who is seventy-two. Not only does Brenda have seven children of her own and fourteen grandchildren, she's also a foster mum who has looked after more than 300 children. What a woman.

Sharon Osbourne presented her with the award. Both of them were in tears. Sharon's daughter, Kelly, was sitting close to our table, and I could see she was choked with emotion, too. She came across to chat with Uri later, and I heard her tell him, 'My mum's pretty wonderful herself.'

After the awards, I told Uri that Gina and I wanted to go shopping in Harrods. 'Would you like to meet the owner, Mohamed Al Fayed?' he asked immediately. 'He's a great friend of mine.' And before we knew what was happening, we were dining in the Harrods' tea rooms and the regal Mr Al Fayed was bearing down on us, with his retinue of bodyguards, to present Ash with a teddy bear.

Chapter Seventeen

I had been following Ann Marie Rogers's court case closely. She took her health authority to the High Court, told the judge that the NHS had sentenced her to death and cited the health secretary's clear instructions that Herceptin was not to be withheld on grounds of cost alone . . . and lost. In February 2006, the judgment went against her.

I was devastated. What Ann Marie felt was probably beyond description. The court case had seemed so straightforward. On 6 February, her legal team set out a compelling argument, asking Mr Justice Bean to declare that Swindon PCT's policy to provide Herceptin only in 'exceptional cases' was illegal. Ann Marie told the judge, 'Waiting for the cancer to return is like waiting on death row. I know that if it comes back it will be terminal. It is hard to put into words the impact receiving the treatment of Herceptin has had on my life.' Her lawyers cited Ann Marie's right to life under Article 2 of the European Convention on Human Rights and the right to respect of her private life under Article 8 – the same clauses that Stephen Grosz had been prepared to quote if my own case had gone to the High Court. And they had an extra weapon, one that hadn't been in my armoury – the health secretary's guidelines. Patricia Hewitt's meaning was 'as clear as could be', the legal team said.

All that the PCT's lawyers could do in reply was offer a flat refusal. Their position was 'not unlawful', their decision was 'not irrational', and they did not accept that 'The failure to fund Herceptin amounts to a risk to the claimant's life.'

The judge's ruling seemed inexplicable. The trust had acted legally, he said, but he gave Ann Marie permission to appeal, and ordered the health authority to continue to fund her Herceptin treatment until the case was heard again at the beginning of April.

Her solicitor, Yogi Amin, said, 'Ann Marie is devastated, but determined to fight on. We believe it is not for trusts to make decisions based on social factors. In essence, this is about managers going over the heads of clinicians.'

In other words, his team was challenging the right of NHS trusts to decide whose life was exceptional and whose was not, whose doctors could prescribe life-saving but unlicensed medicines and who should be denied.

The cancer charities joined in with a chorus of outrage and disappointment, but Jeremy Hughes of Breakthrough Breast Cancer summed it up best: 'It is cruel and unfair for women like Ann Marie Rogers to know that it is money and their postcode that stands between them and this potentially life-saving treatment.'

That week, Roche submitted their application to the European Medicines Agency, requesting a licence for Herceptin as a treatment in early-stage breast cancer. I felt progress was erratic and frustratingly slow, but I was convinced we could sustain this campaign all the way to victory.

And then, on 16 March 2006, I found another lump. The shock was as terrible as the first diagnosis. I felt as though the roof had fallen on my head.

I had been working so hard to help other women with breast cancer, and the knowledge that my own disease could return was an ever-present worry that I pushed to the back of my mind. The growth seemed perfectly round under my fingertips, and I knew it had not been there a few weeks earlier. The mammogram in February had proved that conclusively. But cancers grow fast, and if this was a cancer, I had no right to be surprised. Every doctor, right from the start, had impressed upon me that Herceptin brought no guarantees of long-term remission.

The uncertainty that followed during the next six weeks was almost enough to kill me. I had three biopsies taken, and there was no way of telling what the result would be. All I knew was that this lump was in the same place as the previous one, and it felt similar.

I was scared, and angry. I knew that when the first lump was removed, the surgical team had achieved what, in medical parlance, is termed a 'narrow margin'. I'd been told later that they didn't know exactly where that margin had been because of a problem with the way it had been labeled, and later still I found out that margin was just 0.2 millimetres. Good practice dictates the whole breast should be removed if the margin is less than a millimetre. I was never offered that option. I had a radiotherapy booster instead.

During those days of terrible worry, I forced myself to get on with my life. My brain has a wonderful ability to put things into compartments: my subconscious says, 'I can't deal with that – we'll shove it in a box and we'll deal with it later.' But there's a limit to that technique. Though I kept my worries to myself, making sure I dropped no hint to Richard or Ash, I had to prepare for the worst. I had to assume the cancer was coming back, so that I could deal with it instead of collapsing with shock like the first time.

But there were days when I felt I was walking through a tunnel and there was no light.

A few years ago, when I was in Nebraska, I was talking about Ash's illness to a friend, and I said, 'Sometimes I can't see the light at the end of the tunnel.'

My friend said, 'Barbara, you are the light in the tunnel. You've gone into that tunnel and you've switched on the light.'

Every time I think of that I cry, but not because I'm upset – it moves me because it means so much. Sometimes when you can't see the light at the end of the tunnel, you have to be the light yourself. Make your own light. Shine.

At the beginning of April, Ash and I travelled to London to give moral support to Ann Marie at her High Court appeal. We stayed overnight because Ash wasn't strong enough to do two journeys in a day. I struggle, and he finds it impossible. There were several other children with us, friends of Ash from the hospital, because a day excursion had been planned for them. That worked out well for me –

Ash was due to go with them, anyway, so I tagged along. He had his friends, and I had a friend, their nurse, to talk to on the train.

An early night was on the agenda because we had to be up before 5 a.m. to head off to the *GMTV* studios. After a series of television and radio interviews, I put Ash in a studio taxi to take him to Devon's and I jumped in a black cab and went to the courthouse. As I stepped out of the taxi, it was camera after camera, flashgun after flashgun – when photographers recognise someone, they all pounce. I felt like I was surrounded by the paparazzi.

All that was going on while they were waiting for Ann Marie. I spoke to someone on Yogi Amin's team, met up with another campaigner, Liz Cooke from Bristol, and waited for Ann Marie, who didn't know me by sight, though we knew each other from talking on the phone.

I told every reporter that if the High Court ruled in Ann Marie's favour, it would be a massive verdict: all breast-cancer patients would be entitled to Herceptin. The concept of 'exceptional need' would become irrelevant, and I strongly believed that was as it should be – everybody's needs are exceptional.

I felt I had started the fight, even though it was her court case, and I wanted to see her win. Knowing that Yogi Amin felt she would probably win, my own confidence was high. I wanted to be there at the end, to celebrate with her. It had been my idea to make this a human-rights fight and take it to the High Court, and I wanted to be there giving her support at the finish.

Ann Marie arrived and I walked into the court with her

and Yogi Amin. It was a very special moment. I'd never been in the building before. There were so many corridors – I thought at one stage I'd never find my way out. We walked for miles through the building, and Ann Marie and I both were breathless going upstairs, which is one of the side effects of Herceptin. We went panting up those stairs, and when we got to the top we had to sit down, even though there were hordes of reporters who wanted quotes.

And suddenly one of Ann Marie's lawyers burst through the doors, beaming and punching the air, and told her, 'You've won!'

We both burst into tears and hugged. It was an emotional moment. In many ways, it was even better than winning my own battle, because this time I knew it would be for the whole country.

This moment was critical because of the wording of the three Court of Appeal judges' ruling: it was 'irrational and irrelevant' to say Ann Marie did not have exceptional circumstances. I thought, Nobody can oppose us now. Everybody's going to win.

I felt so frustrated to know that Swindon Health Authority had wasted £300,000 on that court case. That money could have funded so many women's treatment. It was absolutely insane.

I went down the stairs to find cameras everywhere. Someone said, 'How old are you now, Barbara?' and I said I was in my second year of being forty-nine, and did they do airbrushing? That got a laugh.

Ann Marie emerged and read a statement: 'I feel as if I have taken on the world and beaten it, not just for me but for everyone else. I couldn't have asked for a better verdict. I did this for all women battling this dreadful disease.'

Yogi Amin promised the ruling would have 'huge implications' and added, 'The postcode lottery, for Herceptin at least, should no longer exist.'

As he spoke, I looked around at the surge of photographers, camera crews and reporters. This was an extraordinary moment for Ann Marie, but it also marked a crucial step in my own fight. I had been campaigning hard for the moment when the courts would recognise that all human life is exceptional. Finally, that day had arrived, thanks to the united efforts of a great many people. A precedent had been set. The NHS was still not obliged to fund Herceptin for everyone, but after this moment there could be no going back.

Despite our elation, though, my thoughts kept going back to my own situation, and to the result of the biopsies. I still didn't know whether my cancer had returned or not. For the rest of that day I did TV interviews, and whenever the journalists said what good news it was that I was in remission, I had to keep giving the same reply: 'Well, you never know, it's still fifty-fifty whether it'll come back. We just don't know.' Later, I picked up Ash and had a cup of coffee with Devon and Rita, and then headed back to Millbank to do some more TV for the *Six O'Clock News*.

It did help to be so busy, but it was very awkward at times, too. I felt guilty that I wasn't telling them about my new lump, because I have had nothing but kindness from the press. I know everybody moans about journalists, but without the media I would not have been standing outside the High Court that day, telling the world what this case meant – that soon every breast-cancer sufferer in Britain would have the chance of Herceptin, this miraculous drug, on the NHS.

Ash and I went home on the train, and my respite child came to stay. I was keeping myself as busy as humanly possible. No one who hasn't experienced fostering with a disabled child could imagine how busy it is – I work all the time. And that was what I needed. My work was my lifeline: if I stopped working, I would start worrying.

The High Court victory was on 12 April 2006. I wasn't due to get the results of my three biopsies for another fifteen days.

Chapter Eighteen

My wait for the initial ultrasound scan had been long enough, and almost a month had passed since then. I couldn't help remembering the people I'd nursed through their final illnesses. Death from cancer can sometimes be awful. The pain can be hard to control, and one of the most important tasks for a nurse is to make people as comfortable as possible when they are facing death.

If I reach that point, I want the doctors and nurses to do all they can to help me die peacefully. I would always want to die peacefully rather than in terrible pain. Giving large doses of morphine, when all hope was gone, used to be the norm, and I know I would want that for myself.

All the people I had watched die from cancer were at the front of my mind from the day I was diagnosed with the disease myself. Breast cancer tends to go to the bones, and that is one of the most painful cancers there is. There are always people who would like to discuss with you how their relative died. They tell you, 'My mother died of breast cancer – she died in terrible pain.'

I feel like saying, 'Thank you for sharing that with me.' But instead I say, 'Oh dear, that's very sad,' and I try not to take it on board. It sometimes seems as if everybody that has ever had a relative die of breast cancer has shared with me what terrible pain they were in when they died.

I lost a good friend, Jane, in the middle of 2006, and her pain was not well controlled. The doctors always say, 'We can control the pain. You won't be suffering,' but she was in dreadful pain.

She used to say, 'I try not to cry in front of the dogs, because it upsets them.' That broke my heart.

Jane was sixty, but a very young sixty, and she was a good friend in my cancer support group. I was friends with her right through to the end, and that's the difficulty with a cancer support group – you make good friends, but there's always the chance that you will lose them. I couldn't bring myself to go back there for four weeks after she died. It wasn't that I didn't care about the people there – you get close to them. And that hurts.

It's just so sad that Jane had to suffer. She wasn't afraid of dying, but at times her pain was very bad. Nobody wants to go through pain, and she endured a lot of it. The last time I saw her she was in hospital, and she said, 'Oh, Barbara, I wish they weren't so harsh when they tell you you're dying. They just say, "There's nothing more we can do for you, you're dying now. We'll try to keep you comfortable."' Jane asked me, 'Do they have to be so harsh?'

I really think sometimes it was better the way nurses used to do it, when we would give the bad news to the relatives and not the person who was dying, and leave them a bit of hope. Poor Jane didn't have any of that. She just had the harsh realities. She lived on her own, because she'd lost her husband a few years earlier. She deserved better than that.

Realities have a way of looming larger during cancer

treatments. Soon after my diagnosis, a neighbour gave me Gloria Hunniford's book about her daughter, the former *Blue Peter* presenter Caron Keating, who died from breast cancer. It was a hard book to read. I didn't really feel like reading about how somebody died of breast cancer when I had just been diagnosed myself. But I did read it, and I cried my eyes out all the way through.

Caron and Jane were on my mind when I went for the results of my biopsies. The doctor had been optimistic, but I was too worried to feel hopeful. When she first looked at the ultrasound, the doctor had said, 'I think it's a benign lymph node.'

I had retorted, 'You told me that last time and it turned out to be cancer.'

The biopsies had been a fairly serious procedure. I had hoped that nothing more than a needle biopsy would be required, like the previous time, but actually it was a core biopsy, in which comparatively large pieces of tissue are taken. The procedure had been done in three places, which required a local anaesthetic.

'I have a gut feeling it's going to be benign,' the doctor repeated. I didn't believe her. This was the same doctor who'd found the original cancer and said it was a lymph node – and then I'd had the biopsy and gone back an hour and a half later to be told it was cancer.

I've nothing against her at all, because it's very difficult to tell with an ultrasound: sometimes you can tell whether it's cancer, and sometimes you can't. I'd had an unusually round cancer, and cancer is usually irregular. Ultrasounds can be misleading, and it's not lack of knowledge or lack of care. The fact is, cancer isn't a simple disease: it's not as cut and dry as it might seem when you find a lump.

On 27 April, with my heart in my mouth, I went to the hospital at nine o'clock to get my results. I saw the consultant surgeon, Mr Raymus, and, looking at my breasts, he said, 'You've got an excellent cosmetic result. I'm very pleased.'

Never mind the cosmetics, I thought. I said, 'Is it cancer?'

He said, 'Oh, did nobody tell you? There's nothing to worry about.'

I truthfully do not remember much about the rest of that conversation. I do remember I asked to have both breasts removed. I said, 'I want them off. I don't want breasts – take them away.'

He said, 'I'm not doing that. The cancer was under your arm. It would make no difference to remove two healthy breasts and I'm not doing that.'

I went to the car park afterwards and I cried and cried with relief. Then I went to Tesco to have a cup of coffee and calm myself down. The relief was overwhelming.

Chapter Nineteen

The result of that biopsy changed everything for me. It was the difference between life and death, and it freed me to focus all my energy on the campaign. Herceptin was as prominent in the headlines as ever. Up and down the country, new cases were being reported every week of women who knew their lives were precious, no matter what the PCTs said. The first male breast-cancer patient also won the right to the drug from his local trust in Maidstone, Kent. He had been turned down twice by his private health insurer. His case highlighted an important point: anyone can get breast cancer. The vast majority are women: 41,000 new cases a year, compared with just 300 men. But to those 300 and their families, the statistics are irrelevant. Meanwhile, in Shropshire, seven campaigners staged a sit-in at the PCT's headquarters in Shrewsbury: they simply turned up with sleeping bags and refused to leave the reception area. The trust held an emergency board meeting and overturned their earlier decision to withhold treatment for one of the women, Sharon Moore.

I was cheering them on the whole way. They had the determination to fight and the backing of their families. When women act together so emphatically, they are unstoppable. The pressure on NICE seemed certain to force a cave-in sooner than expected, and I was fielding calls from journalists on a daily basis. I was constantly explaining that we had won a major battle at the Court of Appeal but that the fight went on. Deep down, though, I had a feeling that victory was getting closer.

On the afternoon of 11 June 2006, both my landline and my mobile phone started ringing non-stop – the media had heard whispers that NICE was set to make a major statement and they wanted me to comment. Of course, I couldn't offer any comment until the announcement was official. My instinct was to be cautious, but I felt excited as well.

On 12 June 2006, NICE issued their statement.

They announced a draft recommendation that Herceptin should be made available to women with early-stage breast cancer. That meant the drug would be freely available from the NHS, at an annual cost to the health service of £100 million.

The news flashed across the country, and for thirty-six hours my world once again went mad. I was hurled straight into maximum media mode. The amount of organisation required to coordinate dozens of interviews in a day would make anyone's head spin.

Most of the organising had to be done by me because I couldn't rely on the news crews to work together. At the start of my fight, I'd naïvely expected to see cooperation between rival journalists, but I soon learned that this is the last thing they do . . . and I was caught in the middle of the maelstrom.

It's up to me to protect my sanity, so I had to make sure

I knew exactly what I was doing and who was coming. That evening, the phone calls finally stopped at 11.15 p.m. First of all, the crews wanted me to go to Bristol, then they said I had to face the cameras in my home, then they said I had to go to Bristol again. Finally, I put my foot down and said, 'You can all come to me, if you want an interview. You know where my house is by now.'

And they did. My day started the next morning at 4.45 a.m., when a satellite van arrived outside my door, with the generators making a terrible racket. I did a live interview for *GMTV* at 6.20 a.m., followed by another session live at 7.10 a.m. It was unseasonably cold that morning so I was in the garden freezing to death.

I did solid interviews until nine fifteen. At this point, I had to dash out of the house to attend a dance lesson for an hour, learning rumba. North African dancing and belly dancing were fun, but I had not been able to do them for a year: it's difficult to dance with my arms above my head, because of my operation. So I took up salsa and Latin-American. The class was all women and we had tremendous fun.

That morning, I went with Ian, Ash's martial-arts teacher, because he had been telling me how martial arts had given him excellent coordination. I had said, 'Hah! Bet you can't dance.'

He had taken me up on the challenge: 'I'm coming with you to your rumba class.' He struggled, but he was a pretty good sport about it, in front of fifteen women. That afternoon, the phone continued to ring, and the TV interviews went on as well.

In between interviews, I was doing the washing-up, watering and potting plants, making cups of coffee and being filmed as I did it. I was even being filmed while I was being filmed by other television crews. It just didn't stop.

Just before three o'clock, I did interviews with the *Daily Telegraph*, the Press Association and the *Western Morning News*, all of them over the phone – and then Patricia Hewitt rang up. It was uplifting to receive her call, though I will never get used to lifting the receiver to discover there's a Cabinet minister on the other end of the line.

When Ash got home from school, it was time for the madness to stop. I threw some things in a suitcase, dropped the dog off with some friends and took us both to Little Bridge House, the children's hospice in Barnstaple. It had been a manic day and I was worn out. I desperately needed a break, and there could be no better haven than Little Bridge House, where we can stay the night. We got there at quarter past six, just in time to watch the early-evening news on ITV. I went upstairs at 9 p.m. and fell into bed, so exhausted I could no longer stand up.

If I want, I can leave Ash at Little Bridge House and take off for the weekend, but it's a wonderful place, and I love being there with him – that night especially, it was a break for us both. I knew I didn't have to worry about what time Ash had his drugs: I just handed them over to the staff knowing they would look after all of his medication for me.

It was the perfect place to relax and take stock after one of the most extraordinary days I'd had in some time.

Chapter Twenty

Every day people ask me for advice on their struggle to get the right medical care. It's not only the fellow cancer sufferers I meet at my support group – people email me, phone me, write to me, even stop me in the street.

I joke that I should be lecturing to college classes, but there's a serious side to my experience. I had a crash course in fighting cancer and fighting the system. No one gave me a handbook – I had to work out the rules as I went along . . . or make them up.

The main lesson I've learned is to make your fight as public as possible. Don't hold back – no half-measures. Without publicity you can do nothing. If I hadn't had the back-up of the press, I couldn't have made a difference.

Use the media. They can be intimidating, but they are the biggest weapon in a campaigner's armoury. When they fight with you, they are a tremendous asset. The media saved my life. I'm fairly young to have cancer, and that probably worked to my advantage with the media, because it belied the common misconception that cancer is an old person's disease. But I'm old enough to know who I am, and to have the confidence to project that personality. Many of my fellow campaigners are women in their fifties and sixties.

Sadly, women in their thirties often don't even want people to know they have cancer.

I would advise anyone in my shoes to bombard their local MP. I didn't contact Ian Liddell-Grainger at first, because I thought he'd be too busy with weightier matters. He soon put me right. 'My constituents are my whole job,' he said. 'Bridgwater voted for me to be the voice of the town, its advocate. I can't ever be too busy to listen to you. If I let that happen, I'm failing in my duty.'

My MP, I realised, was there to help me, and that went for all the people at the top. When I contacted Stephen Grosz, I didn't think, He's the best lawyer in Britain – much too important for little me. I turned that on its head and thought, He's the best lawyer in Britain – no one else will do.

Stephen won't mind if I add a proviso – I'm a big fan of Cherie Blair. Her speciality is actually employment law, otherwise I might have hired her. That would have been dramatic, and I knew I had to be dramatic with my publicity.

Another key point: make sure your consultant is on your side. If he's not, change consultant. It's not that difficult. You have a legal right to change your consultant if need be. It can be done.

The other thing is to look at hospitals and move if you need to. It's not just Herceptin that is part of the postcode lottery. Scotland, for instance, tends to get drugs before England, and six months can make a massive difference to life expectancy or even survival.

Certainly at one point I thought about moving to Edinburgh because I knew doctors were able to prescribe

Herceptin there. People are loath to move, but in the end, if you're looking at £20,000 for a treatment, it's worth moving to a different area.

Having said that, I've advised hundreds of women to move and not one of them has. It's amazing – they say, 'Ooh, I can't move!' I'd do it!

I tell them, 'Rent a room. Live there on your own if you have to, because as long as you're living there you are entitled to treatment in that area. It's better than being dead at home. Do it to save your life!'

There are so many people who just give up. My advice is: fight on all levels, even when you're not well. I've heard people say, 'Oh, the drug I need is available five miles down the road, but I can't get it here.' So move five miles down the road. It's cheaper to rent a room at £150 a week, which is only £600 a month, than it is to pay £1,400 a month to have a drug on private prescription.

You've got a legal entitlement to move and get care wherever you want, but that right is not made very clear. When I wanted to get treatment in the Royal Marsden, I was told it would have to go to the PCT for funding, which could take up to three months. I didn't have that kind of time because I needed the operation straight away.

I wish I had gone to the Royal Marsden because it would have been worth waiting for a better operation: I had it done in Taunton, and while they completely cut out the cancer, they did it by a very narrow margin. That didn't improve my chances of survival, but it happened because Taunton only has a small specialist breast-care centre and a general surgeon.

No one warned me of that, and I didn't do my research quickly enough – or rather, I allowed the operation to go ahead before I'd finished finding out all the facts. It's not knowing things that does the damage, so I would urge people to go to whatever support groups there are, such as Breakthrough Breast Cancer, and plan the best path forward with caution. If necessary, delay the operation a couple of weeks while you look at your options.

It's important not to panic. Two or three weeks are not going to make a whole lot of difference. Most cancers have been growing well over a year before you actually find them, so wait: get your head around it and then go for the operation. Don't rush.

Join a support group for motivation, because you will always find positive people there to carry you along with them. I still go to CAFE, the cancer support group in Taunton, because on my bad days they carry me through. Most of the time, because I'm a very positive person, I am able to carry other people along.

It's not difficult to make people sit up and listen. 'You've been told that there's no hope? So let's have a look to see how well you can live what's left of your life. Are you entitled to this or that benefit, to this or that holistic therapy? Above all, make the best of what you've got. Because everybody has to make the best of life.'

Friends are terribly important. Don't isolate yourself. There is a temptation to crawl into a hole when you're ill. When I was first diagnosed, I looked at the wall for a fortnight. I couldn't talk to people and I just buried myself in my bed and cried. That is not the way to get better.

Try and share the burden among your friends. You'll find some friends can cope with some things and some can cope with others. I shared my grief with all my friends, rather than overwhelming one of them. That worked.

One more piece of advice: make the most of all the conventional medicines available. These drugs save lives, even if some of them have undesirable side effects. In May, I had to stop taking one of the anti-cancer drugs, Arimidex, because my knees seized up with arthritis and I was walking like the Crazy Frog. The pain was excruciating. I can move my legs more freely now. Arimidex, which can only be used by post-menopausal women, is a more effective treatment than Tamoxifen, but the side effects are worse for some patients. That was certainly the case for me: I couldn't walk. It is essential to retain some quality of life: how could I care for Ash if I was in a wheelchair? With great difficulty, is the answer – I'd manage, but it would be tough. So I'm back on Tamoxifen, and like it or not I will have to take it.

Tamoxifen can also have side effects. It gets rid of oestrogen in your body, which some tumours use to make them grow. I get a lot of joint pain and a lot of hot flushes, which I can live with. A friend of mine says she never has to put the central heating on now. The joint pain is quite annoying, but it was far worse with Arimidex. Tamoxifen isn't the best drug to be on, but it's a lot better than nothing. It's better than being dead.

There are a great many complementary therapies, and they can be pleasant as an extra, to make you feel good, but they don't make you better.

I do believe a meat-free diet reduces the risk that the cancer will come back. I've tried very hard to do that with my diet – I'm eating much more sensibly. What's essential is to constantly bear in mind that a diet cannot prevent or cure cancer on its own. It helps, but it's not everything.

I asked my oncologist about my diet and he replied that if he had breast cancer he would certainly want to avoid milk and dairy produce, but he couldn't say that there was any sort of conventional medical back-up, because the theory has never been tested properly.

People turn to complementary cures because they don't have full confidence in conventional medicines and the NHS. That has to be addressed. The health service isn't going to get away with providing substandard care as long as there are people like me and Jayne Sullivan, my good friend and partner in crime.

Jayne is an astonishing personality: bouncy, hysterically funny and unfailingly upbeat. I've never met anybody like her – she is a ball of fire.

She contacted me in 2005 to say she'd seen me on TV talking about how the PCTs in Wales weren't even testing Welsh women for HER2 factors. The reporter asked what message I would give to Welsh women with breast cancer. I said, 'Please, if you do nothing else, get yourself tested. See if you are HER2 positive. It is vital to save your life. More than this, Wales needs a Welsh campaigner.'

Jayne was watching, and she demanded a test from her doctors – they didn't want to test her, but she insisted and sure enough she was HER2 positive. She rang me up and said, 'I'm going to fight this with you. I'm right by your side. I'm going to stage a protest by sleeping in the Welsh Assembly.'

Nobody else could have done that. Jayne is such a bundle of live energy. We met in London, when we appeared on *This Morning* together. My first thought was what a stunningly good-looking woman she was.

Jayne actually knew when she went to protest in the Welsh Assembly that she had got Herceptin, but she still protested for other women. And that's what makes her special: she is out there, fighting for everyone.

She lived and slept in that building under the gaze of the press, day and night, with the cameras on her, for six days. She would go out to the toilets and ring me, because she wasn't allowed to use her phone inside, and she'd say, 'I'm going mad! I'm going bonkers!'

But builders who were working there were bringing her bottles of wine – she'd call and say, 'We're going to have a party.' And the police were wonderful to her, bringing her in sandwiches. They were all supportive, but only Jayne could do something as dramatic as that.

And only Jayne could have been so successful, because as a direct consequence of her campaign, Herceptin was made available on the NHS for all women in Wales.

Jayne motivates people who need motivation. She came up to the Houses of Parliament with me in June 2006, because I'd nominated my MP, Ian Liddell-Grainger, for the Patsy Carlton Award with Breakthrough Breast Cancer. No one could wish for a better MP than him. If he was Monster Raving Loony Party I'd still vote for him. He's motivated about everything. He's a fighter and he fights with me, so when I found there was an award for people who helped with cancer, I knew he had to win it. I not only recommended him but I rang them up every day until he got it. He, together with so many other people, helped save my life.

Chapter Twenty-One

For the first time in more than a year, I found myself able to think about the rest of my life. I had been fighting for my future day by day for so long that it seemed almost eccentric to be making long-term plans. Now I felt strong enough to make some decisions.

I decided to learn new skills. I'm self-employed, so it's up to me whether I use those skills – for now, it's enough that I explore new ideas in my career. One was inspired by a medical technique I had discovered during chemotherapy: when I lost my hair, I had my eyebrows replaced by semi-permanent makeup or micro-pigmentation, a sort of light tattoo, by a beautician, because without eyebrows or eyelashes anyone would look ill.

The beautician had explained she had a long waiting list, with more work than she could handle, because so many women wanted the confidence boost that her art could give. I loved the idea of providing a service that made women with cancer feel good about themselves, so I decided to train as a paramedical make-up artist. Whether I will ever use that skill professionally, it's too early to say, but I was fascinated by the possibilities. As well as eyebrows and eyelash enhancement, a medical make-up artist does aureolas and nipples, for people who've had full or partial mastectomies. If a woman has a breast removed, the nipple is taken off in most cases, and this is often intensely distressing. This make-up, though cosmetic, can make a significant psychological difference. Aureolic reconstruction creates a very realistic appearance with a 3D effect. Women who have endured the ordeal of breast cancer leading to mastectomy can be made to feel whole again by this process, which is carried out post-reconstructive surgery. This final touch gives women their confidence and dignity back.

These treatments are all quite expensive, so I intend to carry them out at cost to help women with cancer. I discussed this with my friend Majella Norris. She used to be a solicitor, but she had breast cancer in both breasts, and after that felt she couldn't stay in the legal profession any longer because it was so stressful. She has since retrained to be a beautician. That's the kind of lateral thinking which inspires me. I never saw myself doing medical cosmetic work before the cancer, but then again, I never imagined that I would meet Cherie Blair, or that Ash and I would one day watch Trooping the Colour from 10 Downing Street.

I met Cherie Blair before I collected the *Sun*'s Wonder Mum Award as part of the prize. I discovered she was a good listener and a likeable woman. That's often the way when you encounter people you've only read about in the papers – it's often a pleasant surprise to meet them in person.

Cherie worked her way through the room, shaking the hands of all the wonderful mums. When she reached me, I said, 'While you're here, can I speak to you in private?' I told her about Ash and how ill he had been, because I knew he'd love to meet her, too.

She called over her secretary, had a quiet word and arranged there and then for us to be the prime minister's guests at Trooping the Colour in June.

Cherie came across as down-to-earth and level-headed. She joked about not wanting to have her photograph taken with all the mums, because we all looked so glamorous, she said. Of course, we got a great photo of the whole group.

My visit to Downing Street with Ash was even more enjoyable. It's hard to impress a twelve-year-old, but Ash really was impressed. We took the train to London the night before Trooping the Colour, in mid-June, and stayed in the Jolly St Ermin's Hotel in Westminster, because I felt it would be too exhausting for Ash to travel on the same day – we had to be at Downing Street by 9.30 a.m.

I was expecting ferocious security, but the police didn't even look at the passports and ID documents in my hand-bag. There was one small difficulty straight away, though: we apparently had different invitations from everyone else. As we walked up the street, with a crowd of other people, an official looked twice at our gilt-edged card and said, 'I've not seen one like that.'

I said, 'It is a genuine invitation. It's from Cherie!'

Luckily, one of the policemen knew it was the real thing and let us through. It would have been awful to be turned away on the doorstep.

We went through the scanners and still no passports were being checked; we followed the crowd and ended up in the big square. I realised I didn't have any suntan lotion on, and because I've had chemotherapy I burn very easily. I hadn't realised it was going to be outside – in fact, I was sure I'd been told we would be inside, so I asked one of the guards.

'You shouldn't be here,' he said. 'You're supposed to be watching it from Ten Downing Street.'

So we went back round the house and in through the front door of number 10 – there are huge offices and rooms behind that famous black door, and massive banqueting rooms. We were led straight through to the garden. Suddenly, Ash and I were standing with all the diplomats.

Before long I had started conversations with the mums and dads. It doesn't matter to me whether I'm talking to an ambassador or a waiter – if they've got children I want to hear all about them.

We had soft drinks, and then all the children were taken into the state rooms of 10 Downing Street. The adults walked through to the big square, but I followed Ash indoors. It was a very hot morning and I felt sorry for the Queen – it must have been miserable for her.

I hadn't realised that Downing Street backs on to Horse Guards Parade. I was able to watch Trooping the Colour from the state-room windows on the top floor, with the most fantastic view. There's a small garden behind number 10, and on the other side of the fence we could see all the guards in their bearskins.

We could see the Queen quite clearly, and I was quite surprised that there were women among the troops and in the band. Ash watched with me, enthralled – the staff put a video on for the youngsters in case they were bored, but Ash watched the parade from start to finish.

At the end, everybody came through. I had asked if we could possibly have a photograph of us with Tony Blair. We were told there was no chance – it wasn't done, they said – but one of the staff had a camera, and as everybody came in we were pulled to one side, met Tony Blair, shook his hand, had a photograph with him and then had a photograph taken with Cherie Blair.

Tony Blair didn't say a lot, simply that he was delighted to meet me and he'd been following my fight. It was very formal. He spoke for longer to Ash, but I might never find out what was said! Ask Ash what they discussed and he says, 'Nothing much,' as twelve-year-olds do. For all I know, the prime minister confided his resignation plans in Ash, but that's a scoop we'll never hear.

Not long after the trip to Downing Street, we went on holiday to Turkey with the Cosmos vouchers I had won at the Tesco Mum of the Year Awards. Ash and I deserved a holiday, and to know that the holiday company was footing our bill made it even more relaxing. The Cosmos director chose our destination, an upmarket holiday village with beautiful scenery and infinity pools overhanging the sea. The food and the staff were wonderful – Ash and I spent the rest of the summer talking about the most fantastic two weeks of our lives.

Chapter Twenty-Two

At the end of August 2006, NICE issued the statement I had worked so hard to hear: Herceptin would be made available on the NHS to all women in the early stage of HER2-positive breast cancer. We'd known since June that this decision was expected, but I was still thrilled. The chief executive of NICE, Andrew Dillon, was writing to all PCTs, telling them they should withhold the drug only where doctors had concerns about the health of a patient's heart. He said, 'Our assessment of Herceptin shows that it is clinically and cost-effective. The guidance has been issued rapidly to ensure consistent use across the NHS.' He could have added that the decision had been fast-tracked only after intense campaigning and the intervention of the health secretary.

Patricia Hewitt could count it as a personal victory, just as much as me: 'This is a very important decision for breast-cancer patients,' she said, 'and I welcome the final guidance by NICE on the use of Herceptin. It removes any uncertainties that might have remained in the NHS about the clinical- and cost-effectiveness of the drug. It means all PCTs must provide funding for this treatment within the next three months if they are not already doing so.'

To celebrate, I went on Sharon Osbourne's teatime chat show on ITV, which had been launched that week. Sharon is one of my heroes – she fought cancer, which is now in remission, and she's an outspoken, opinionated woman who isn't afraid to have fun, work hard and promote the causes that matter to her. She's a great mother, too. When we met at the *Sun* Wonder Mum Awards, we hit it off immediately, and I was delighted that she chose me to be one of her first guests. 'You're a life-saver,' she said on air, and that meant more to me than she could guess. Ash was in the audience, grinning and cheering.

The relentless publicity had evidently had an effect on NICE. At the beginning of September, the watchdog announced it was going to try to find NHS savings by identifying treatments that were, in fact, a waste of public money. The health minister, Andy Burnham, pointed to the £11.5 million spent every year on antibiotics for children's sore throats that are usually caused by viruses – antibiotics have no effect on viruses. He also cited unnecessary tonsillectomies and hysterectomies, which cost £21 million annually. 'It won't solve the financial crisis,' he said frankly, 'but it could help.'

Two days later, on 9 September, the final resounding victory in the Herceptin campaign was won by Liz Cooke from Bristol. She had been preparing to fight Bristol North PCT in the Court of Appeal, and a judge ruled that because she would have won her case, the PCT should pay her legal costs of around £40,000. This emphasised how emphatic our success had been. I felt we didn't just win the battle on points – we triumphed in every round.

At the beginning of October, my victory was rewarded with a series of prestigious awards and invitations. *Best* magazine announced I had been named one of the Bravest Women in Britain. That delighted me because it recognised that my campaign had been focused on helping all women with breast cancer. I was also invited to the Woman of the Year lunch, and I had an opportunity to tread the catwalk at the Breast Cancer Care Fashion Show at the Grosvenor House Hotel, in a wonderful outfit. All the clothes were donated for the night by Europe's leading fashion designers, and my friends Jayne Sullivan and Majella Norris were in the audience, cheering me on. In the same month, I was asked to address a group of MPs at the Breakthrough Breast Cancer Fly-In at Westminster, and to give a talk, from a patient's perspective, to the British Oncology Pharmacy Association. I was even asked to open a Cancer Research shop in Minehead! There was no time to rest on my laurels.

All this activity feeds my energy levels. The more I have to do, the more I manage to fit in and the better I cope. If I need to do something, I'll find ways of doing it. Robert, my ex, said to me when I was first diagnosed, 'Oh dear, Barbara, now you're ill you'll only be able to run at a hundred and ten per cent.' He knows what I'm like.

I needed every ounce of energy, mental and physical, for the fight of my life. I had never expected to have to address an audience, or debate with lawyers, or give an interview on camera. I had never wanted to be a celebrity – nursing was my vocation, though I didn't understand that until my mid-twenties.

I have a talent for what psychologists call 'cognitive therapy', which means looking at things in a different way. If

I'm low, I force myself to reorder my thoughts until they're cheerful and positive. I've done it for years. When I was training to be a nurse, I was given short sessions outlining different therapies. One of these was cognitive therapy, and a light went on in my head – I thought, What a good idea, and ever since, I've tried to wear a happy face. I don't mean I walk down the street grinning inanely, but I am conscious of my expression: I can either have a frown and a miserable face or I can lighten up the way I look. People smile at me and I smile back, and I feel happier. It's all about trying to keep myself buoyed up as much as possible. I'm not an evangelist for positive thinking, I don't insist that everyone must think the way I do, but it is one of the ways I deal with life's crises.

I tried to smile all the way through my treatment. I smiled when I went in to see the nurses, I smiled with gritted teeth at the people who stood in my way, I smiled at everybody for everything – because the more you smile, the more people smile back at you.

When Americans say, 'Have a nice day now,' some British people would say that sounds false. But I say, 'Oh, thank you! That's really kind. I will. You have a nice day, too!' I listen to them and I mean it.

Perhaps I have a naïvety about the world, but Ash has got it as well. We smile a lot and we laugh a lot. Richard, however, is serious-minded. It takes more to make him laugh. I've had Ash and me laughing beyond control, in those fits of giggles that you can't stop, and then Richard starts laughing, too.

Of course, there are times when sadness and grief weigh

too heavily and I have to give in to tears. This summer, I gave a very tearful talk at the children's hospice in Taunton. Before I went up to the stage the organisers were talking about a child who had died – he had planned his own funeral. I was sitting there trying not to cry, because I had to go and give my talk, but I was already wobbly. I started talking about Ash and I burst out crying. I was a complete failure as a speaker that day, but afterwards people said my tears had said more than words ever could.

My philosophy is simple: nobody's life is worth more than any other. However young or old you are, whatever you do, however much money you have in your savings account, you are the same as everyone else: a human being. I know what I've been through, and nobody's going to tell me I don't matter; but I also know everybody else matters, and I will not let other women and men go under.

There are still advances that need to be made. To this day, in fact, not all centres are testing women to see if they are HER2 positive. Whatever money is left in my fund will be distributed to people who are caught up in the postcode lottery, and not only those who are fighting breast cancer. My struggle is not about breast-cancer care; it's about all the care that is not good enough and is better elsewhere in the world. The turning point for me came with the ruling that I could have Herceptin because of 'exceptional need'. I went from protesting that my life did have worth, and that I knew I was worth saving, to asking why I was more worth saving than anybody else.

I'm in this campaign for ever now. It's not what I was expecting two years ago, but who really knows what will happen next in their life? It's not so very long since I thought I'd settled down and could look forward to a life with no more traumas and dramas. And since then my existence has been a rollercoaster ride with no brakes.

But in a strange way, the sheer speed of the change has helped me to slow down. All my life I've been rushed, and now I'm not. Time is what Herceptin has given me. My specialist, Dr Bryant, has warned me more than once that all the drug can do for me is 'buy time'. What else would you buy? There's very little point in buying a new handbag, is there? 'Would you like some time, Mrs Clark, or would you prefer to have your fingernails done?' I have to laugh.

Before I had cancer, I had been tired for years, pushing myself on and caring for other people instead of putting myself first. That's the norm for every carer, every nurse. I spent all my time working and never had time to stop and appreciate things.

But since my diagnosis, I sometimes feel almost like a child again. I'll stop now and look at the way the sun is gleaming off the bonnet of the car. I notice silly things that I once would not have dreamed of looking for. It wouldn't have occurred to me that I had the time. Now I'm going to enjoy what's left to me.

Most of all, I'm going to enjoy my children.

I like to think I'm good at being a mum, because we have the freedom to have lots of fun. If I want to nip to Paris for a weekend, we just get our tickets and off we go. I've tried to teach my boys that spontaneity, because I go along with the proverb that says our children are like arrows shot from a bow – we can guide them, but we can't fly with the arrow.

One of the best side effects of my illness is that it's brought me and Richard much closer. He was hard work as a teenager – though no worse than the average, because I think all teenagers can be difficult. But when I was diagnosed it was as if somebody had waved a magic wand and he took responsibility. He became a man, and it was absolutely wonderful to behold. The stroppy teen vanished and he changed back to being my old Richard, the persona he had been when he was younger. He's turned out to be a wonderful young man and I'm so proud of him.

After those difficult teenage years, he was super, and has been ever since. I'm even allowed to kiss him in public.

I went into Brandon's Tool Hire, where he works, to get some carpet shampoo today, and he said, 'Give me a kiss, Mum!' In front of his colleagues! What a difference from his teens, when it was, 'Kiss me in public? How dare you! You're so humiliating!'

I see a lot of him now. He lives just down the road, and he comes back at least twice a week with his washing and a sheepish expression, saying, 'I love you, Mum . . . Do my washing, Mum?'

Ash is a very laidback boy, a gentle, kind boy. I've come across so very many children in my work, but Ash is different, a miniature grown-up. He has social skills way beyond his age. He may be a little behind in schoolwork – and it is only a little, about a year or so, despite all the time he's spent in hospital – but he cares so deeply about other people. He has incredible empathy.

He had this gift right back when I first started caring for him. When he was four years old, and I'd just taken him on, he went through a nasty stomach bug and for several days I was nursing him day and night. It was pretty tiring. Anyone who has had to look after a poorly four-year-old will know what I mean. When he was on the mend, I flopped down on the settee, and I must have looked shattered because he came up to me and said, 'You look tired, Mummy. Make yourself a cup of coffee and I'll get you a mat for it.'

That's unusually considerate in a four-year-old – most children that age wouldn't notice if you were tired. He always has done, and he cares. He'll say, 'Are you all right, Mum? I'm here for you, Mum.'

Almost all his school reports comment on how socially aware he is, and how he's a peace-maker. He'll step between two children who are fighting and sort them out in a non-violent way. He wants to be a teacher when he grows up.

He's got a lot of love to give, despite all the upheavals in his life. Coming to terms with them has been difficult for him, but he's so aware of his emotions – and I can't claim it's all down to me and the upbringing I've given him.

I don't think he notices being poorly. He's been ill all his life, and it's all he knows. When I was having chemotherapy, I used to think, Gosh, this is what Ash must feel like all the time. He's never known what it's like to feel normal and that's a sobering thought. He's never known what it's like to wake up in the morning not full of medication. He lives with the nausea and he thinks that is the way we naturally live. That's what I surmise, because he certainly never complains.

I don't make a big deal of his illness with him. If he ever says, 'I don't feel very well,' I just say, 'Never mind, you'll feel better later. Have a lie-down.' I don't run around after him, because I am determined that he must not see himself as an invalid.

Being ill has also made me see his illness differently. We have always talked about death and dying – probably many people would disagree with me, but Ash knows about his illness and I believe there's no point hiding that from him. If he wants to talk about it, we do.

My illness has given me much more of an understanding of how he feels, and how he has to cope with knowing. I know that however many drugs and medications I'm on, the cancer will probably kill me in the end. There's almost no doubt that with such an aggressive cancer I am not going to live a very long life.

But I've got used to that knowledge, and I know now, or at least I understand better, how Ash copes. It's just something we're going to have to accept, and we get on with our lives. Ash has always enjoyed life so much. He's always so full of life. Now I know why: since I have been ill I've enjoyed life so much more.

That certainly was not what I had expected, but I find I've been a lot happier since the diagnosis of cancer. I don't mean during the initial weeks, because obviously I was devastated, but right the way through my chemotherapy, when everybody else, healthy or not, was three or four out of ten, on a normal day I was at least a seven or an eight!

And while I'm wearing my smile, I've got my wonderful boys around me – Richard and Ash. I can put an arm round each of them and hug them to me. Simply to be alive, and able to do that, is the most wonderful thing in the world.

About Breakthrough Breast Cancer

Breakthrough Breast Cancer is the UK's leading charity committed to fighting breast cancer through research, campaigning and education. We have established the UK's first dedicated breast cancer research centre, in partnership with The Institute of Cancer Research. The Breakthrough Toby Robins Breast Cancer Research Centre, housed in the Mary-Jean Mitchell Green Building, is associated with the Royal Marsden Hospital, at the very heart of the largest cancer complex in Europe.

Our research focuses on understanding the causes of breast cancer, finding better ways to detect the disease, identifying more effective and gentler treatments, and understanding how to prevent breast cancer.

Our campaigning and education work aims to raise the profile of breast cancer, to fight for the best possible treatments and services for everyone, and to increase awareness and understanding of the issues surrounding the disease. Our Campaigns and Advocacy Network (Breakthrough CAN) is made up of individuals and organisations who aim to make a difference to breast cancer services, treatment and research by campaigning for improvements.

The Generations Study

If breast cancer is to be prevented its causes must be found. In September 2004, Breakthrough Breast Cancer, in partnership with The Institute of Cancer Research, launched The Breakthrough Generations Study, the largest and most comprehensive investigation ever undertaken into the causes of breast cancer. Spanning over 40 years and including over 100,000 women from all walks of life, it will investigate why some women develop breast cancer and how it may be prevented in present and future generations. We need to raise £12 million to support the first 10 years of the study.

If you would like to find out more about the work of Breakthrough Breast Cancer or make a donation visit www.breakthrough.org.uk or call the Breakthrough Information Line on 08080 100 200 8am-8pm Mon-Fri and 9am-12noon on Sat.

Most breast cancers are detected by women who report unusual changes to their doctor. This highlights the importance of being breast aware.

So the message from Breakthrough Breast Cancer is simple:
Show your breasts some TLC!

Touch. Look. Check.
Touch your breasts. Feel for anything unusual.
Look for changes. Be aware of their shape and texture.
Check anything unusual with your doctor. Chat with your friends if you are worried.

There is no need to follow a fancy routine for examining your breasts, just be familiar with how they look and feel so that you notice changes. You can do this by looking and feeling in any way that makes you feel comfortable – in the bath or shower, when dressing, standing or lying down. If you find anything unusual or are worried, you should talk to your GP.

Changes to look out for include:
- Size or shape, e.g., one breast might become larger or lower than the other.
- Skin texture such as puckering or dimpling of the skin.
- Appearance or direction of nipple, e.g., one nipple might become inverted (turned-in).
- Discharge: one or both nipples might discharge a blood-stained liquid.
- Rash or crusting of the nipple or surrounding area.
- Lump in the breast or armpit.
- Lumpy area or unusual thickening of breast tissue that doesn't go away after a woman's period.
- Pain in part of the breast or armpit that is unrelated to periods.

Remember that nine out of ten breast lumps are not cancerous.
For further information visit www.breakthrough.org.uk or call the Breakthrough Information line for FREE 8am-8pm Mon-Fri and 9am-12noon on Sat.